Railway Clearing House

Atlas of
London 1935

Ian Allan
PUBLISHING

First published 1935 by the Railway Clearing House
This impression 2001 by Ian Allan Publishing

ISBN 0 7110 2789 7

© this impression Ian Allan Publishing 2001

Published by Ian Allan Publishing

an imprint of Ian Allan Publishing Ltd, Hersham, Surrey KT12 4RG.

Printed by Ian Allan Printing Ltd, Hersham, Surrey KT12 4RG.

Code: 0106/B2

INTRODUCTION

This, the fourth in Ian Allan Publishing's new series of railway atlases, reproduces the 1935 edition of the Railway Clearing House *Official Railway Map of London and its Environs.*

The Railway Clearing House (RCH) was established in 1842 to facilitate inter-company payments for through traffic when more than one of the many separate independent railways, eventually numbering in excess of 120, was involved. For this, accurate maps of lines owned by each company, with detailed distances, were required. George Bradshaw produced early maps between 1839 and 1845 but then concentrated on timetables. An RCH employee, Zachary Macaulay, then produced the first station map in 1851, issued by Smith & Ebbs, with subsequent editions; a list of stations was also produced. From 1862 two further employees, Henry Oliver and John Bockett, developed this into the *Handbook of Stations*, which continued, produced by Oliver and Airey from 1872.

John Airey, another employee, broadened the range of maps, producing books of Junction diagrams, including distances, from the mid-1850s up until 1894. In 1895 he sold his business to the RCH, which continued production until 1935. Airey also produced a small map of England and Wales in 1877. In 1896, the RCH produced a large map of the railways of England and Wales, this time in association with McCorquodale, which continued until the 14th edition of 1947. For a detailed history of the maps of Macaulay, Airey and the RCH see *Railway Maps and the Railway Clearing House*, published by Brunel University Library in 1986.

The first book of Junction Diagrams was produced by Airey in 1867 and contained 84 diagrams from across the country. It soon became evident that this was not wholly satisfactory for complicated areas with a multiplicty of junctions within a small area, so in 1869 Airey designed and produced a large diagram, at 1 inch to the mile, covering the Manchester area. It measured 15 x 22 inches and was coloured by hand.

This was followed, in November the same year, by the *Railway Diagram of London and its Suburbs.* Railway developments ensured that new editions of this map followed rapidly, almost yearly until the turn of the century, but then slowed appreciably as the network stabilised. Postwar, maps appeared only in 1919, 1921 and 1927 with a final edition in 1935 by which time the title had been modified as shown above; it is this which is reproduced here. At that time, the railway map of London was as yet incomplete, with lines such as the SR's Chessington branch yet to open. By the time of this map, however, the LPTB had been formed and its railways are shown uniformly, but it had yet to institute its New Works Plan, under which it was to take over some branch lines from main-line companies.

The map was produced in colour to a scale of 2 inches to the mile (1:31,680) as 45 sheets on a cloth back, so that it could be folded flat, between hard covers. These sheets have been assembled and compiled into an atlas format (resulting in the title block being split over maps 3 and 4), but, where the pages do not match the original sheets, there may be some inconsistencies, and an index is now provided. Goods stations are marked as such, and station names are as in use in 1935. Each railway was shown in a distinctive colour and the main railways were shown as follows: GWR — yellow; LNER — blue; LMS — red; SR — green. Lines of the newly-formed LPTB were shown in purple. Joint railways received hatched lines in the colours of the owning companies, except that lines with multiple ownership, such as the West London Extension and East London lines were shown in pink, as were the lines of the Port of London Authority. Other private networks were shown in outline with their appropriate names.

In the Index, where 'Junction' appears in a station name, it is spelt in full, but where it refers to a location, it appears as 'Junc'. Sidings are abbreviated to 'Sid'.

This atlas is a direct facsimile of the original, and any errors present are therefore reproduced as such.

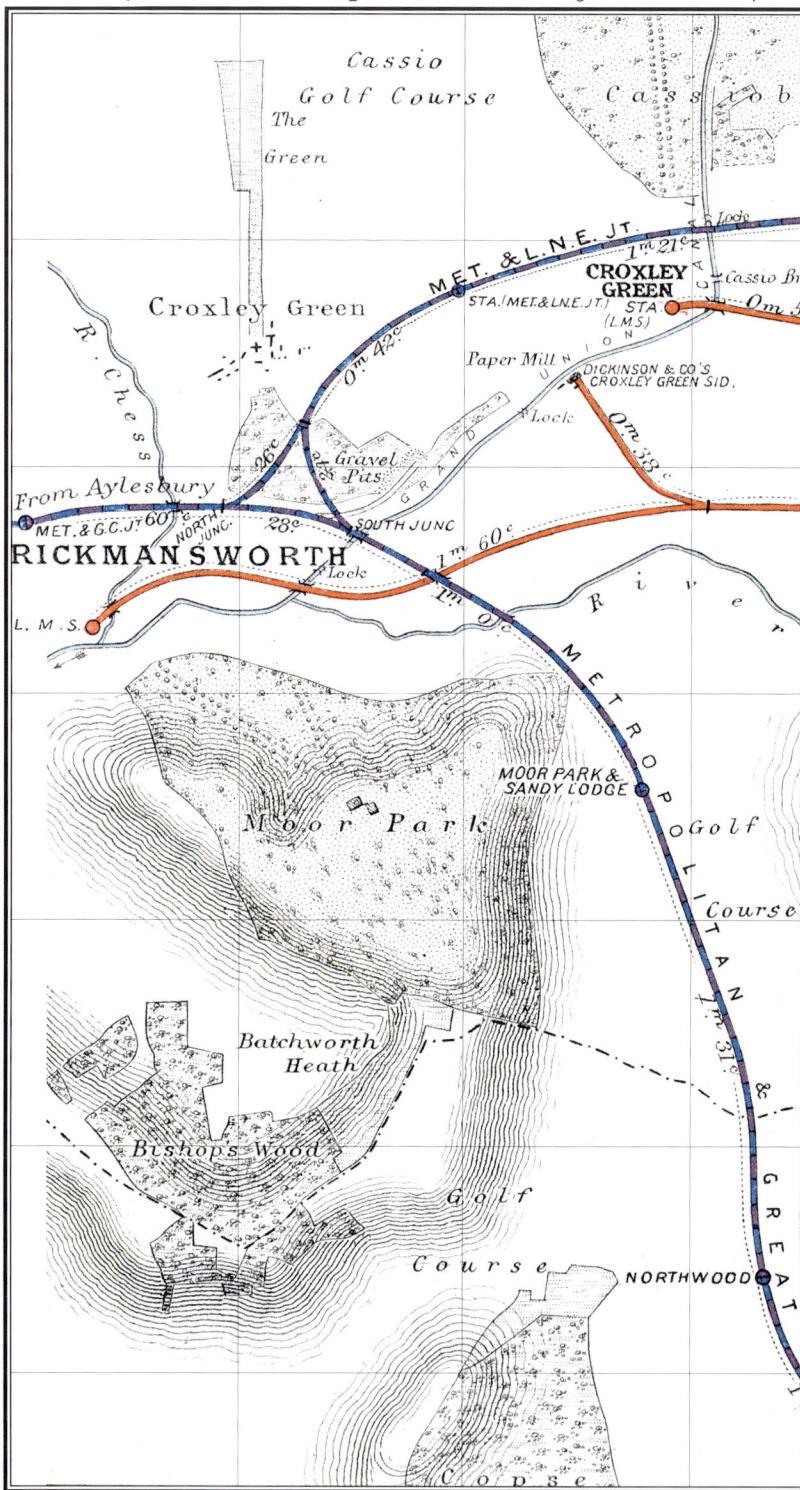

1   2   3   4

A

Cassio
Golf Course

The
Green

C a s s i o b

B

Croxley Green

MET. & L.N.E. JT.

1m 21c

CROXLEY GREEN

STA.(MET.&L.N.E. JT.)

STA.
(L.M.S.)

0m 5

+ T r

0m 42c

Cassio Br

R. Chess

Paper Mill

DICKINSON & CO'S
CROXLEY GREEN SID.

Lock

26c

Gravel Pits

0m 38c

Lock

From Aylesbury

MET. & G.C. JT. 60c

NORTH JUNC.

28c

SOUTH JUNC.

1m 60c

C

RICKMANSWORTH

Lock

1m 0c

R i v e r

L. M. S.

M E T R O P

Moor Park

MOOR PARK &
SANDY LODGE

Golf

D

Course

1m 31c

E

Batchworth
Heath

I T A N

Bishops Wood

&

Golf

G R E A T

F

Course

NORTHWOOD

G

C o r s e

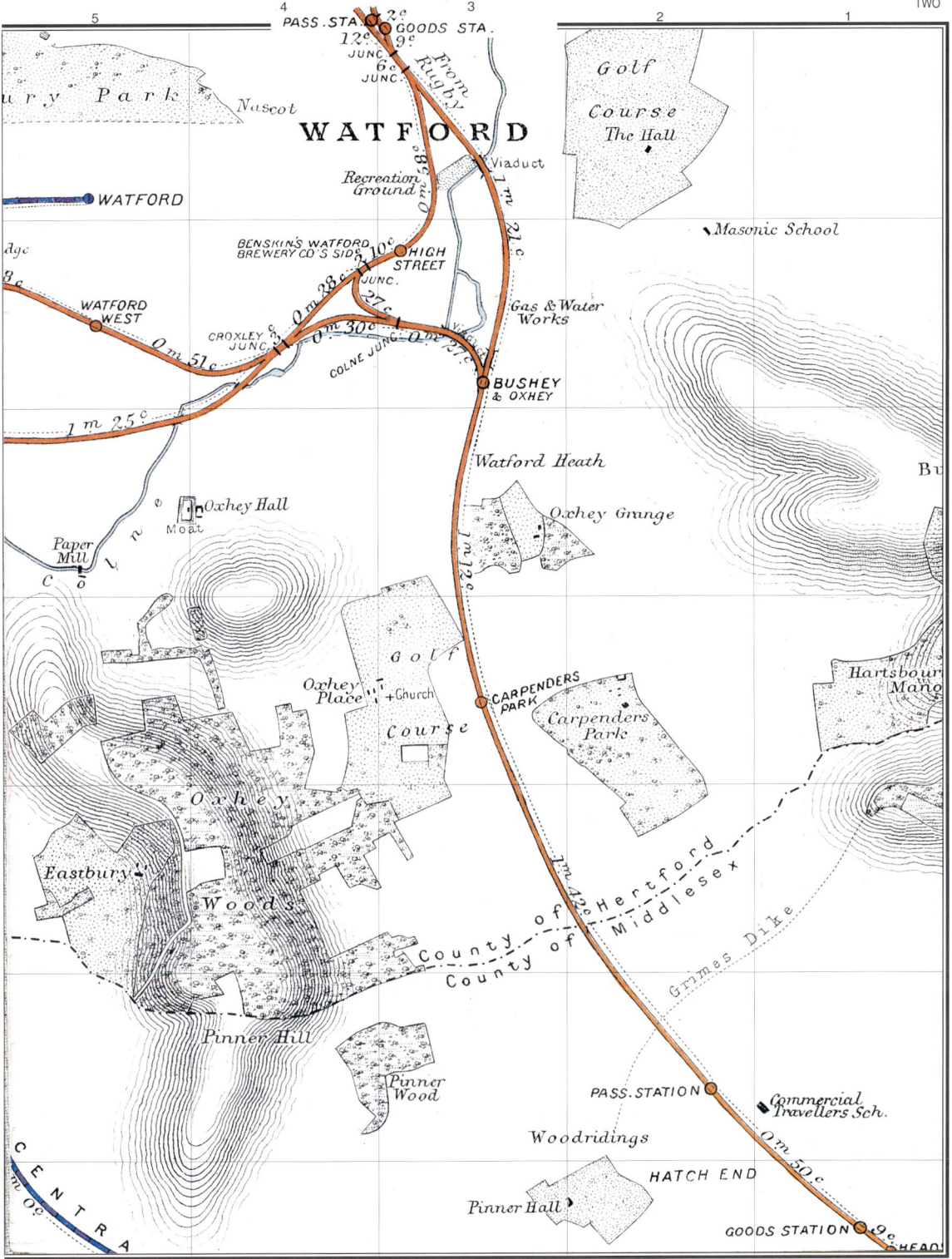

5 4 3 2 1

PASS. STA. 12ᶜ GOODS STA.
13ᶜ 9ᶜ
JUNC. 6ᶜ
JUNC.

From Rugby

Golf
Course
The Hall

WATFORD

Nascot

A

WATFORD

Recreation
Ground

Viaduct

1 m. 21ᶜ

Masonic School

BENSKINS WATFORD
BREWERY CO'S SIDE 10ᶜ HIGH
STREET

0 m. 28ᶜ

JUNC.

0 m. 27ᶜ

B

dge
8ᶜ

WATFORD
WEST

0 m. 51ᶜ

CROXLEY
JUNC.

0 m. 30ᶜ

COLNE JUNC.

0 m. 27ᶜ

Gas & Water
Works

BUSHEY
& OXHEY

Bu

1 m. 25ᶜ

Watford Heath

C

Paper
Mill

Oxhey Hall
Moat

Colne

1 m. 12ᶜ

Oxhey Grange

Oxhey
Place   + Church

Golf

Course

CARPENDERS
PARK

Carpenders
Park

Hartsbour
Mano

D

Oxhey

Eastbury

Woods

1 m. 12ᶜ

County of Hertford
County of Middlesex

Grimes Dike

E

Pinner Hill

Pinner
Wood

PASS. STATION

0 m. 50ᶜ

Commercial
Travellers Sch.

F

CENTRAL

1 m. 0ᶜ

Woodridings

HATCH END

Pinner Hall

GOODS STATION   9ᶜ

HEAD

G

1   2   3   4   5

A

B

LONDON AND

PREPARED AN
AT
RAILWAY CLEARIN

19

C

hey Hea

STATUTI

0   ¼   ½   ¾   1

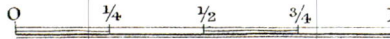

Drawn and engraved b

The distances indicated on this Map are appr

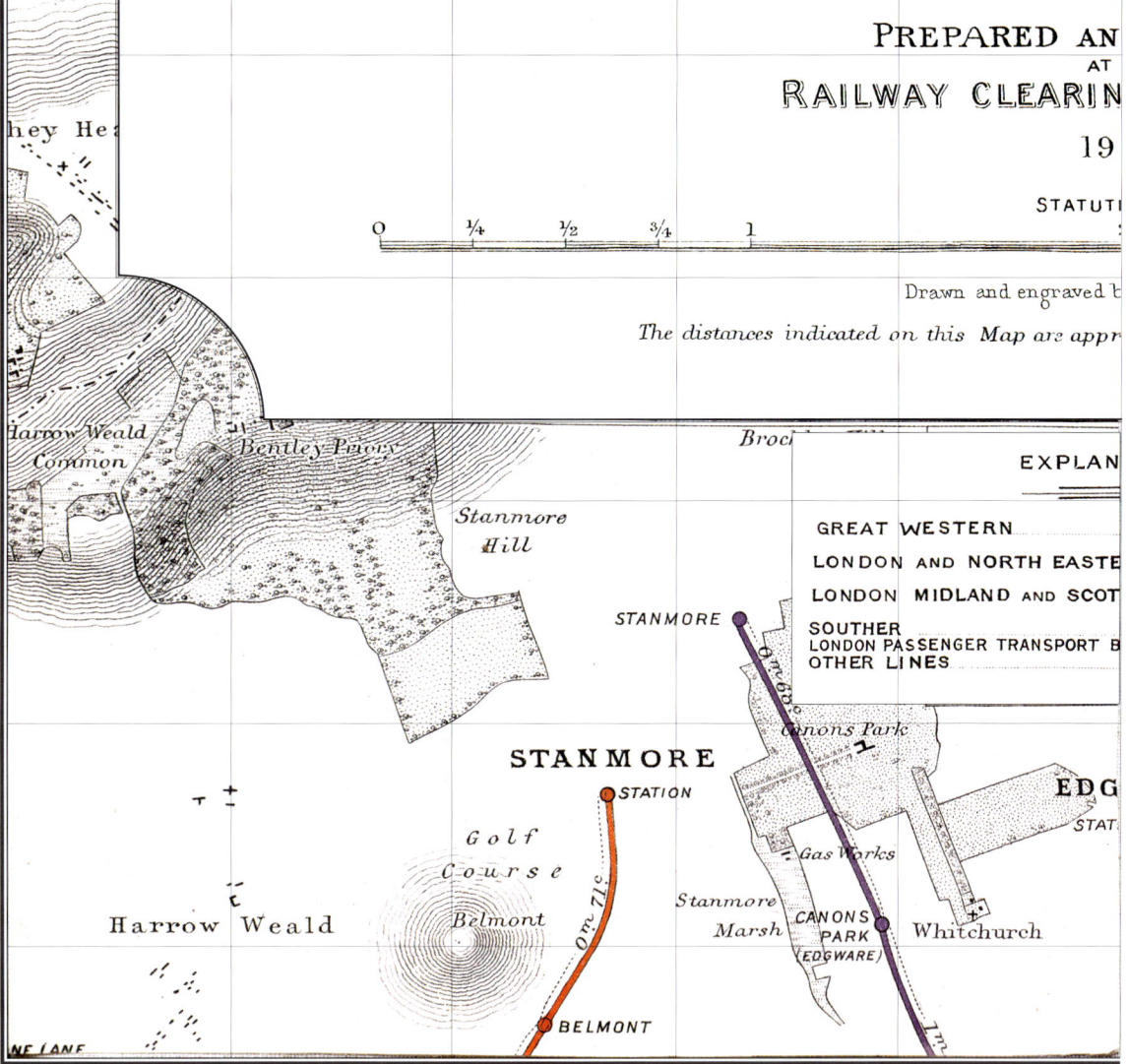

D

Harrow Weald
Common

Bentley Priory

Broc

EXPLAN

GREAT WESTERN

Stanmore
Hill

LONDON AND NORTH EASTE

LONDON MIDLAND AND SCOT

E

STANMORE

SOUTHER
LONDON PASSENGER TRANSPORT B
OTHER LINES

Canons Park

0m 6c

STANMORE

EDG

STATION

STAT

F

Golf
Course
Belmont

Gas Works

Stanmore
Marsh

CANONS
PARK
(EDGWARE)

Whitchurch

Harrow Weald

0m 7½c

1m

BELMONT

NE LANE

G

5   4   3   2   1

A

ITS ENVIRONS

B

d PUBLISHED

THE

G HOUSE, LONDON

C

35

MILES

2   3   4

y J. & W. Emslie, London.

oximate ; their accuracy is not guaranteed.

D

ATION

YELLOW

RN   BLUE

TISH   RED

OARD   GREEN
    PURPLE
    AS INDICATED
    BY NAME

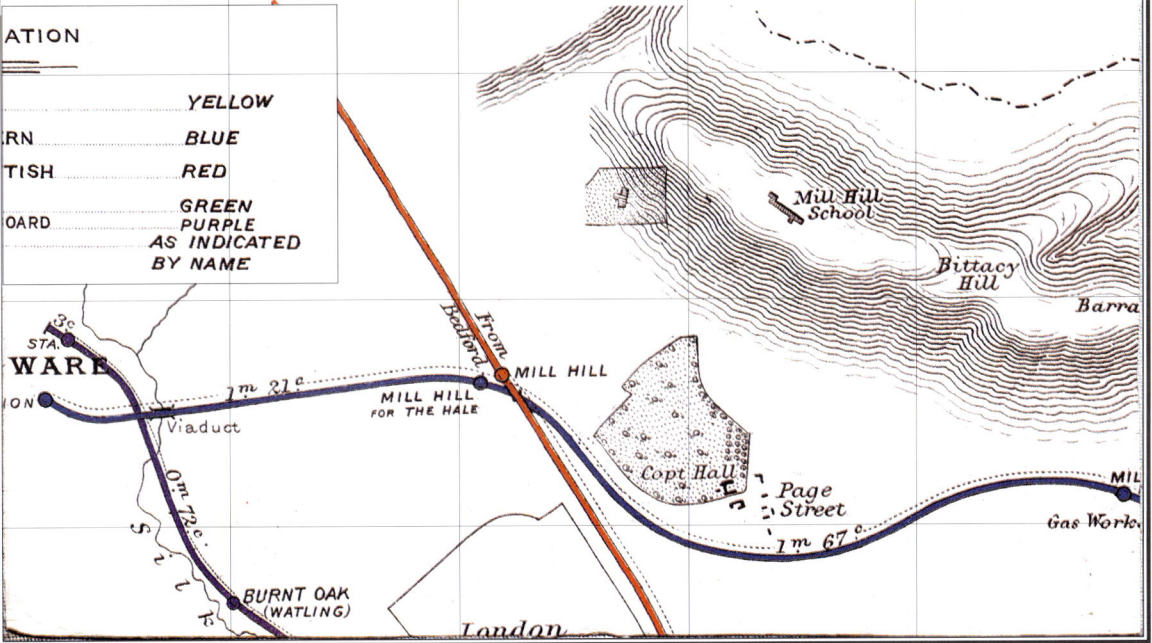

E

Mill Hill
School

Bittacy
Hill

Barra

From Bedford

3c
STA.
WARE
ON

1m 21c

Viaduct

MILL HILL   MILL HILL
FOR THE HALE

Copt Hall

Page
Street

MIL

Gas Work

F

0m 72c

Silk

1m 67c

BURNT OAK
(WATLING)

London

G

1 2 3 4 5

A

Hadley Green

Hadley Common

Trent P...

B A R N E T

HIGH BARNET

Cock Fosters

E...

COCKFOSTER...

From Peterborough

NEW BARNET

B

County of Middle...

County of Hertfo...

1m 48c

0m 62c

C

OAKLEIGH PARK
FOR EAST BARNET

East
Barnet

Copped Hall

Totteridge Green

TOTTERIDGE
& WHETSTONE

Whetstone

Tunnels 1m 73c

D

Dollis Brook

0m 76c

Great Northern Cemetery

Friern Barnet

E

Friary Park

WOODSIDE PARK
FOR NORTH FINCHLEY

0m 48c

North Finchley

NEW
FOR...

Colney Hatch Asylum

F

WEST FINCHLEY

0m 55c

L HILL EAST (FOR
MILL HILL BARRACKS)

Viaduct 0m 68c

G

Victoria Rec^n Ground

Finchley Common

Friern Barnet

5   4   3   2   1

Chase Side

Silver Street

ENFIELD

A

from Hertford

GOODS   PASS.
ENFIELD CHASE

ENFIELD TOWN

Plea Gr

Pleasure Ground

Golf

ENFIELD WEST

South Lodge

B

0m 50 c

0m 47 c

JUNC
GRANGE PARK
STA

Course

BUSH HILL PARK

68 c

1m 13 c

0m 52 c

0m 67 c

Chase Side

C

Grovelands

WINCHMORE HILL

SOUTHGATE

1m 13 c

R i v e r

D

Tunnel

Southgate

1m 18 c

L
ED

HIG

Broomfield Park

PALMERS GREEN
& SOUTHGATE

E

Pa

N e w

Weir Hall
Moat

SILVER STREE
FOR UPPER EDMONTON

ARNOS
GROVE

SOUTH GATE & FRIERN BARNET
COLNEY HATCH

0m 75 c

0m 63 c

0m 62 c

F

MOUTH
OF TUBE

Tunnels

BOUNDS
GREEN

BOWES PARK

WHITE HART LANE

G

1m 37 c

57 0m

Park

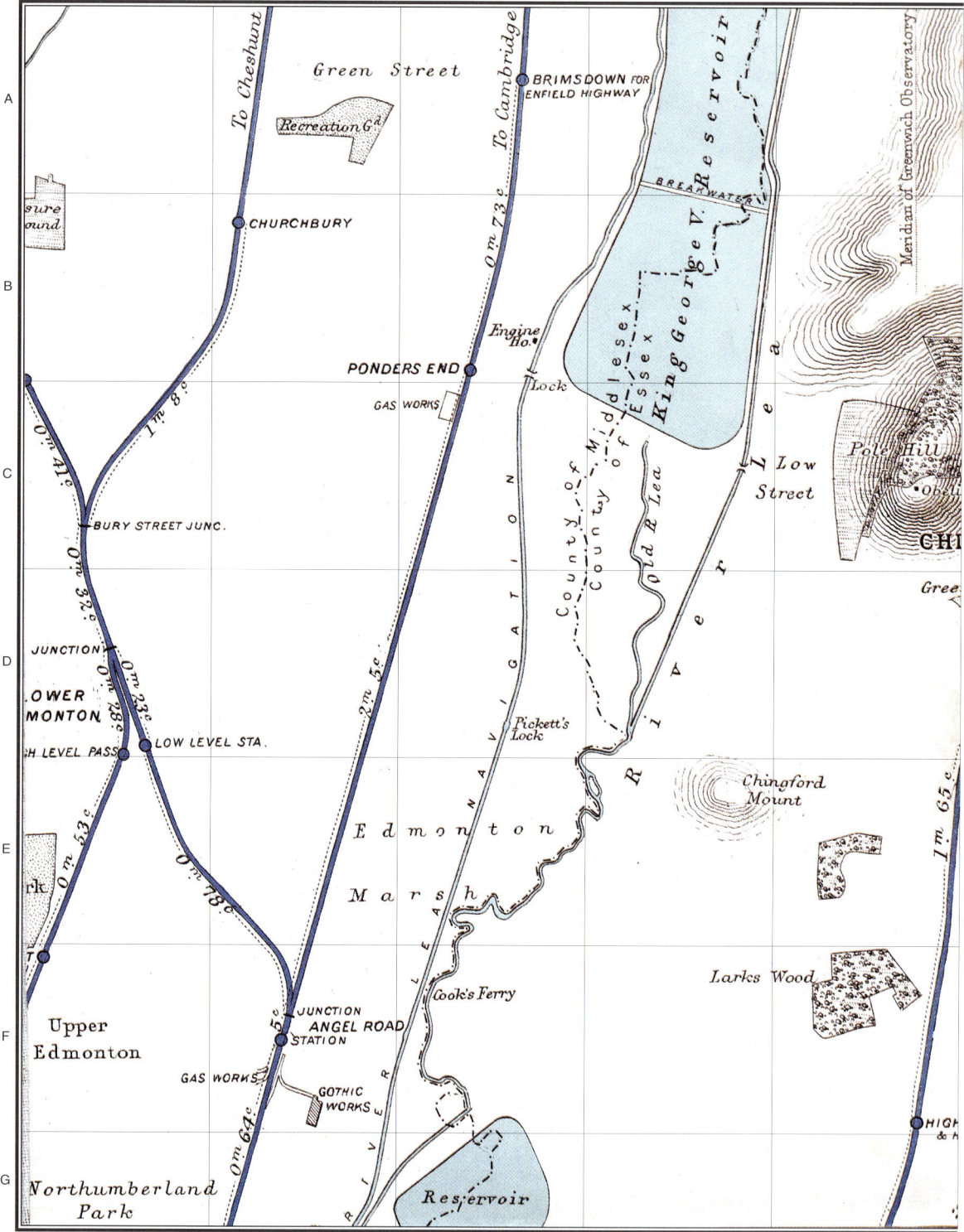

1 2 3 4 5

A

Green Street

To Cheshunt

Recreation Gd.

BRIMSDOWN FOR
ENFIELD HIGHWAY

To Cambridge

0ᵐ 73ᶜ

King George V. Reservoir

Meridian of Greenwich Observatory

sure
ound

CHURCHBURY

BREAKWATER

B

Engine
Ho.

PONDERS END

Lock

GAS WORKS

County of Middlesex

County of Essex

Pole Hill

1ᵐ 8ᶜ

0ᵐ 41ᶜ

Old R. Lea

CH

C

BURY STREET JUNC.

0ᵐ 33ᶜ

2ᵐ 5ᶜ

*Low
Street*

Gree

0ᵐ 23ᶜ

D

JUNCTION

LOWER
MONTON

0ᵐ 28ᶜ

Pickett's
Lock

River

Lea

*Chingford
Mount*

gh LEVEL PASS

LOW LEVEL STA.

0ᵐ 53ᶜ

1ᵐ 65ᶜ

E

rk

0ᵐ 78ᶜ

E d m o n t o n

M a r s h

Larks Wood

T

NAVIGATION

LEA

F

*Upper
Edmonton*

JUNCTION
ANGEL ROAD
STATION

Cook's Ferry

RIVER

HIGH
& H

GAS WORKS

0ᵐ 5ᶜ

GOTHIC
WORKS

0ᵐ 64ᶜ

G

*Northumberland
Park*

Reservoir

RIVER

5 4 3 2 1

High Beech

Goldings Hill

A

Sewardstone

Fairmead
Lodge

B

LOUGHTON

GOODS

1ᵐ 28ᶜ

PASS.
JUNC.

The Warren

C

Golf

Connaught
Water

Course

0ᵐ 77ᶜ

River

Queen Elizabeth's
Hunting Lodge

NGFORD

STATION

F   O   R   E   S   T

D

BUCKHURST HILL

B

Chingford
Hatch

ords
Bushes

E

Golf

Woodford
Wells

1ᵐ 47ᶜ

Course

WOODFORD
JUNC.

0ᵐ 60ᶜ

0ᵐ 55ᶜ

F

AMS PARK
ALE END

Highams

Woodford
Green

Woodford
Bridge

Hale End

WOODFORD

G

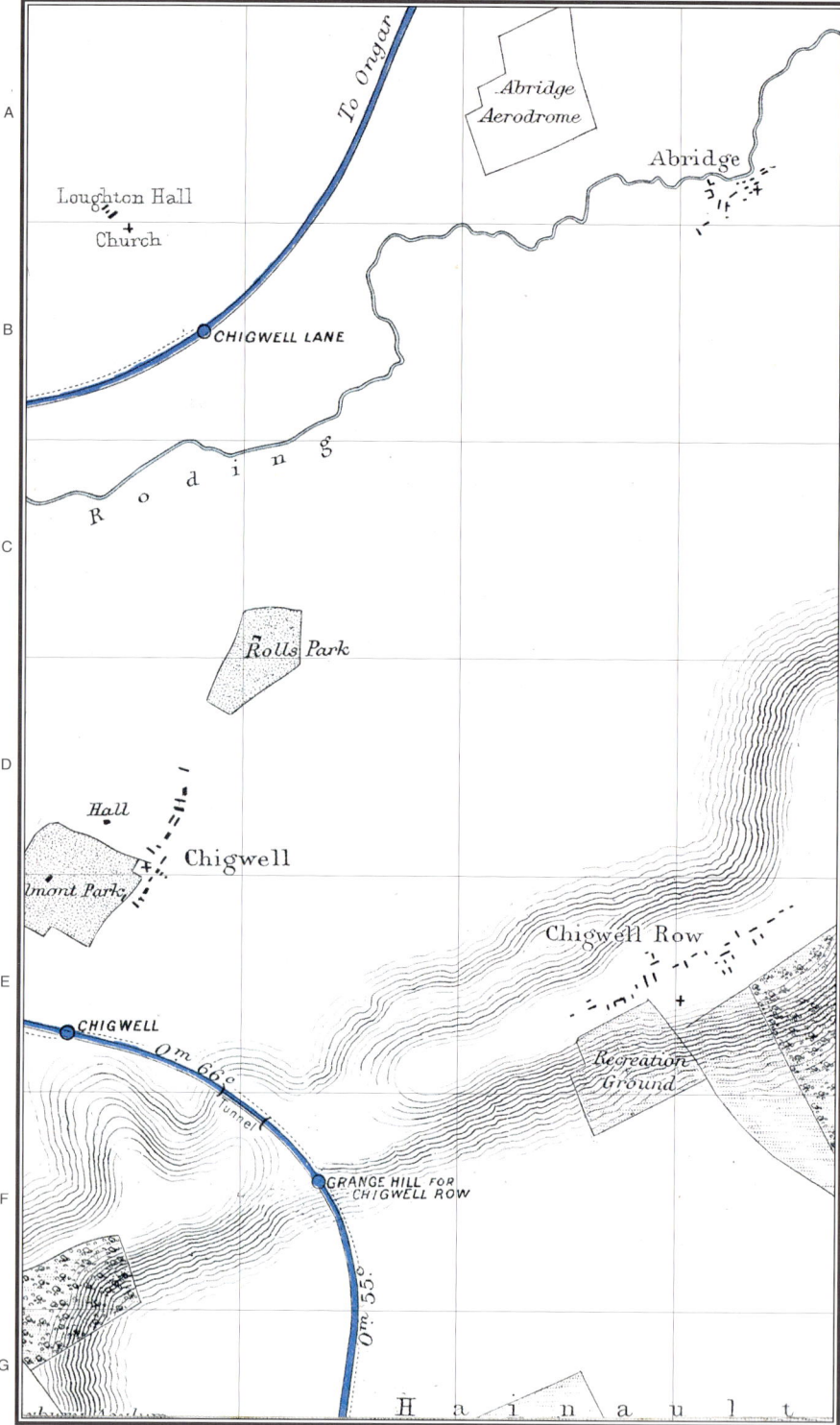

1   2   3   4

A

To Ongar

Abridge Aerodrome

Abridge

Loughton Hall
+ Church

B ● CHIGWELL LANE

R   o   d   i   n   g

C

Rolls Park

D

Hall ●

+ Chigwell

mont Park

Chigwell Row

E ● CHIGWELL +

Om 66'c *Tunnel*

Recreation Ground

F ● GRANGE HILL FOR
   CHIGWELL ROW

Om 55'c

G

H   a   i   n   a   u   l   t

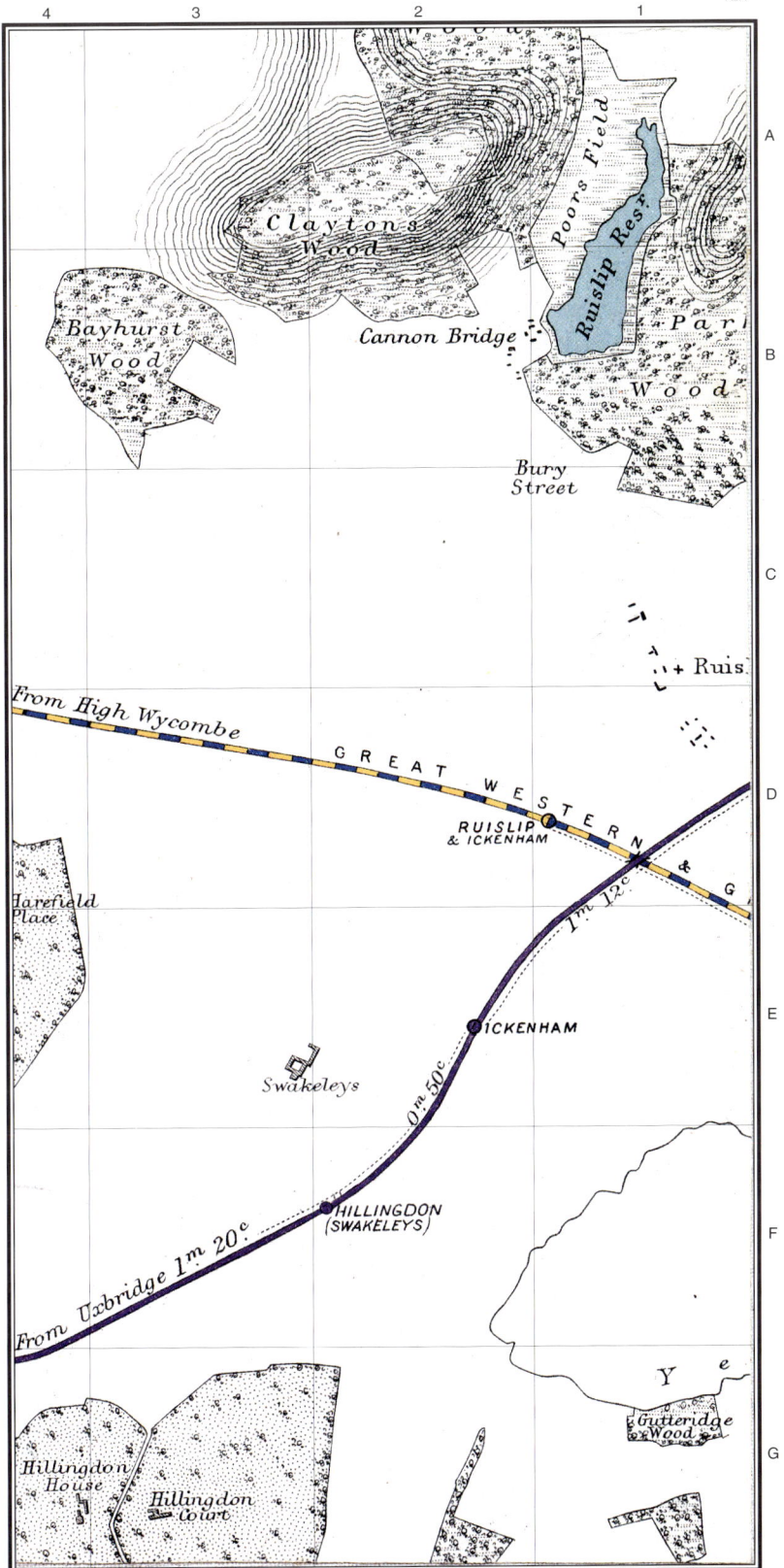

4   3   2   1

A

Clayton's
Wood

Poors Field

Ruislip Resr.

Bayhurst
Wood

Cannon Bridge

Par

B

Wood

Bury
Street

C

+ Ruis.

From High Wycombe

G R E A T   W E S T E R N

D

RUISLIP
& ICKENHAM

& G

Harefield
Place

1ᵐ 12ᶜ

E

0ᵐ 50ᶜ

ICKENHAM

Swakeleys

Y   e

F

From Uxbridge 1ᵐ 20ᶜ

HILLINGDON
(SWAKELEYS)

Gutteridge
Wood

G

Hillingdon
House

Hillingdon
Court

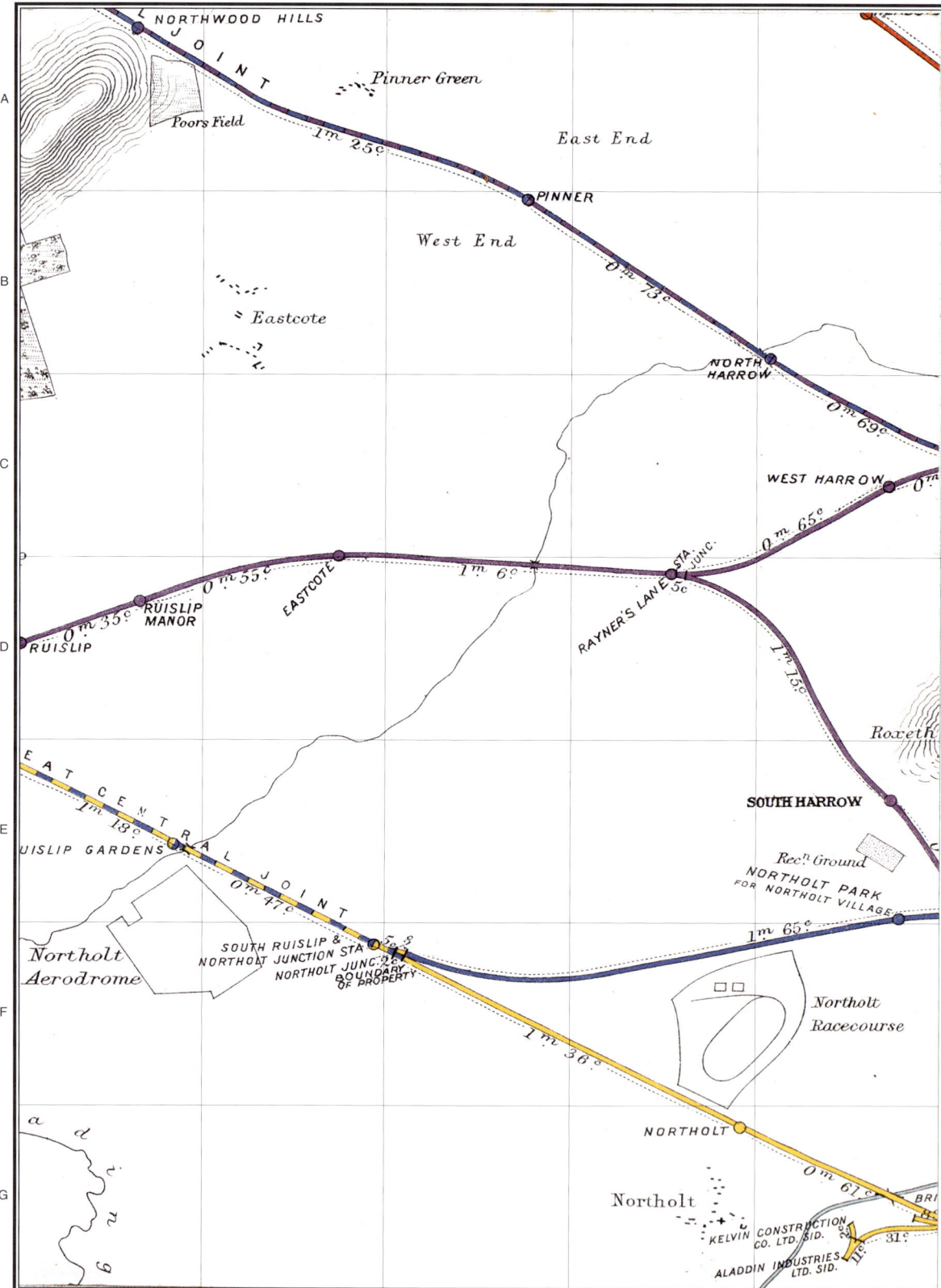

NORTHWOOD HILLS

JOINT

Pinner Green

Poors Field

East End

1m 25c

West End

PINNER

0m 73c

Eastcote

NORTH HARROW

0m 69c

WEST HARROW

0m

0m 55c

EASTCOTE

1m 6c

0m 65c

RUISLIP MANOR

0m 35c

RAYNER'S LANE STA.
JUNC.
5c

RUISLIP

1m 15c

Roxeth

EAT CENTRAL JOINT

1m 18c

SOUTH HARROW

UISLIP GARDENS

0m 47c

Rec.n Ground

NORTHOLT PARK
FOR NORTHOLT VILLAGE

1m 65c

Northolt Aerodrome

SOUTH RUISLIP &
NORTHOLT JUNCTION STA.
NORTHOLT JUNC.
BOUNDARY
OF PROPERTY

5c

Northolt Racecourse

1m 36c

NORTHOLT

0m 61c

Northolt

BRI

31c

KELVIN CONSTRUCTION
CO. LTD. SID.

ALADDIN INDUSTRIES
LTD. SID.

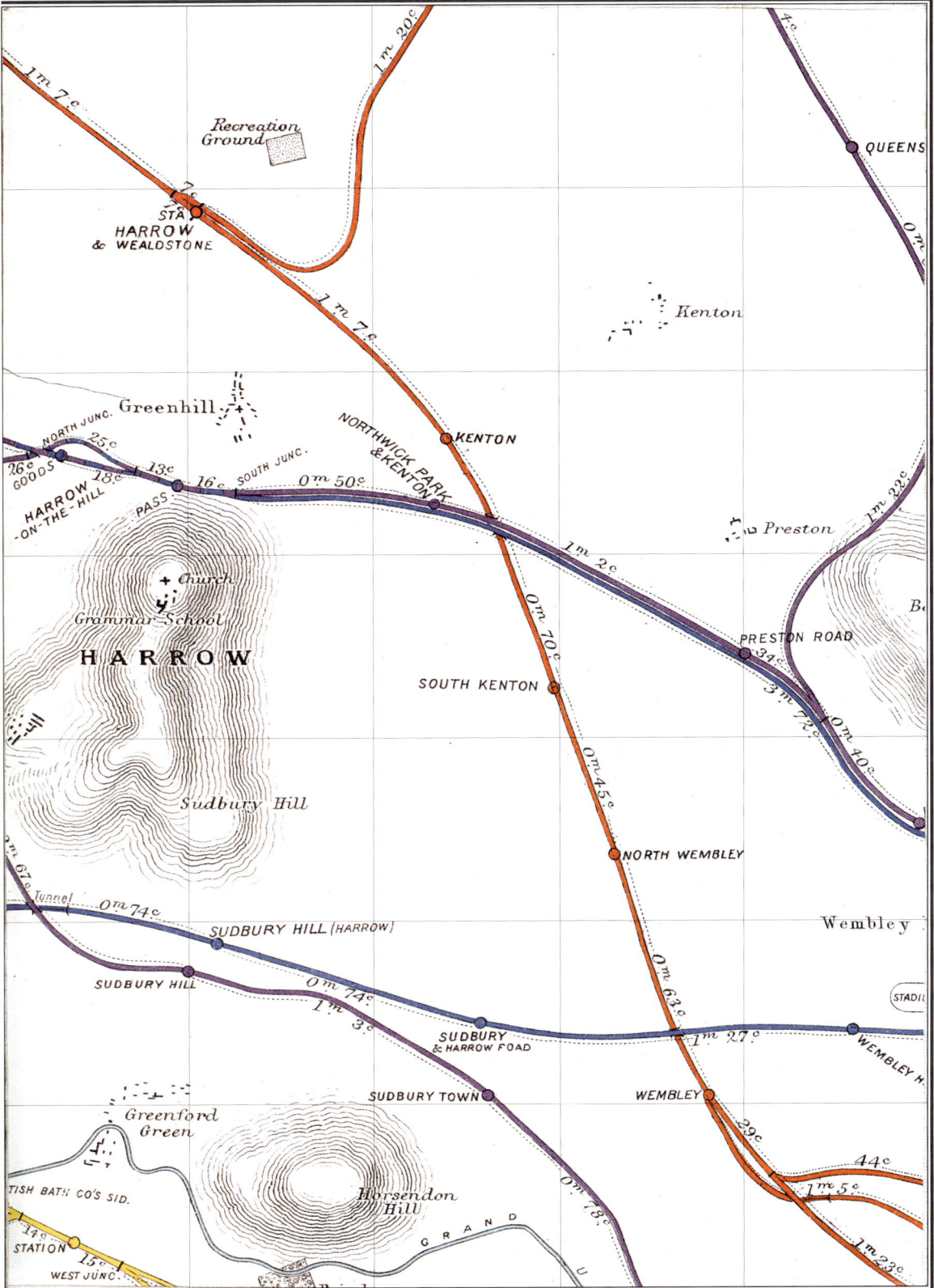

5   4   3   2   1

A

Recreation Ground

QUEENS

1 m 20 c

1 m 7 c

4 c

0 m

B

7 c

STA

HARROW & WEALDSTONE

1 m 7 c

Kenton

NORTH JUNC.

25 c

Greenhill

26 c

GOODS

18 c

13 c

16 c

SOUTH JUNC.

0 m 50 c

NORTHWICK PARK & KENTON

KENTON

C

HARROW -ON-THE-HILL

PASS

Preston

1 m 22 c

1 m 2 c

Church

Grammar School

HARROW

0 m 70 c

PRESTON ROAD

34 c

D

Sudbury Hill

SOUTH KENTON

0 m 45 c

3 m 7 c

0 m 40 c

Be

E

NORTH WEMBLEY

0 m 67 c

Tunnel

0 m 74 c

SUDBURY HILL (HARROW)

Wembley

STADI

SUDBURY HILL

0 m 74 c

1 m 3 c

SUDBURY & HARROW ROAD

0 m 63 c

1 m 27 c

WEMBLEY H.

F

Greenford Green

SUDBURY TOWN

WEMBLEY

29 c

44 c

Horsendon Hill

0 m 78 c

1 m 5 c

G

TISH BATH CO'S SID.

14 c

STATION

15 c

WEST JUNC.

GRAND

U

1 m 23 c

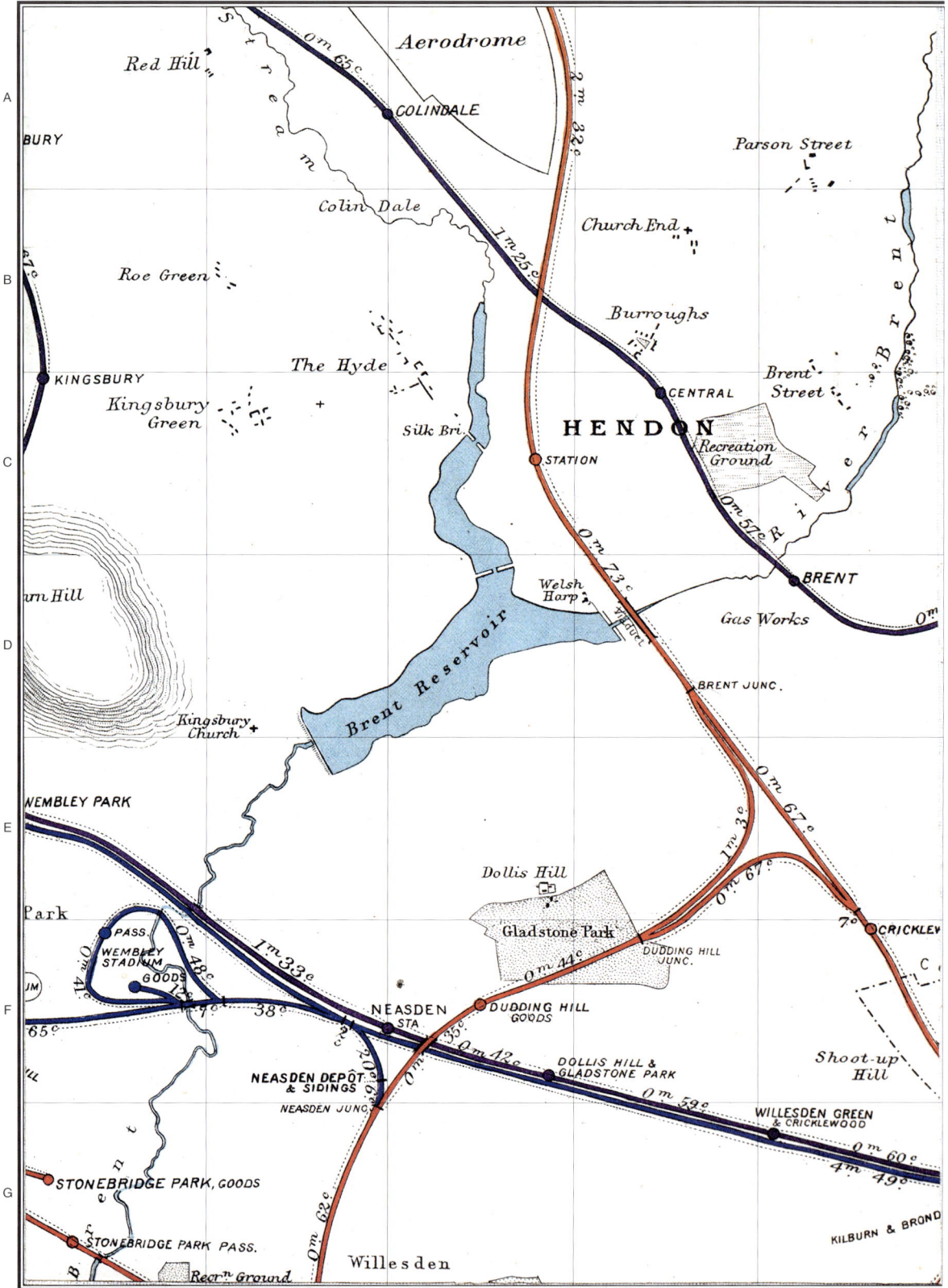

1 2 3 4 5

A

Aerodrome

Red Hill

COLINDALE

Parson Street

BURY

0 m 65 c

2 m 32 c

Colin Dale

Church End

1 m 25 c

B

Roe Green

Burroughs

Brent
Street

KINGSBURY

The Hyde

Silk Bri.

CENTRAL

HENDON

Recreation
Ground

Kingsbury
Green

C

STATION

0 m 57 c

BRENT

0 m 73 c

Welsh
Harp

Gas Works

0 m

n Hill

Viaduct

D

Brent Reservoir

BRENT JUNC.

Kingsbury
Church

0 m 67 c

WEMBLEY PARK

E

1 m 3 c

Dollis Hill

0 m 67 c

PASS.

Gladstone Park

7 c

CRICKLEW

0 m 48 c

WEMBLEY
STADIUM

DUDDING HILL
JUNC.

C

0 m 41 c

GOODS

0 m 44 c

UM

1 m 33 c

Shoot-up
Hill

65 c

38 c

DUDDING HILL
GOODS

F

NEASDEN
STA.

DOLLIS HILL &
GLADSTONE PARK

0 m 35 c

NEASDEN DEPÔT
& SIDINGS

0 m 42 c

0 m 59 c

WILLESDEN GREEN
& CRICKLEWOOD

NEASDEN JUNC.

0 m 60 c

4 m 49 c

STONEBRIDGE PARK, GOODS

G

0 m 62 c

KILBURN & BROND

STONEBRIDGE PARK, PASS.

Recrⁿ Ground

Willesden

5   4   3   2   1

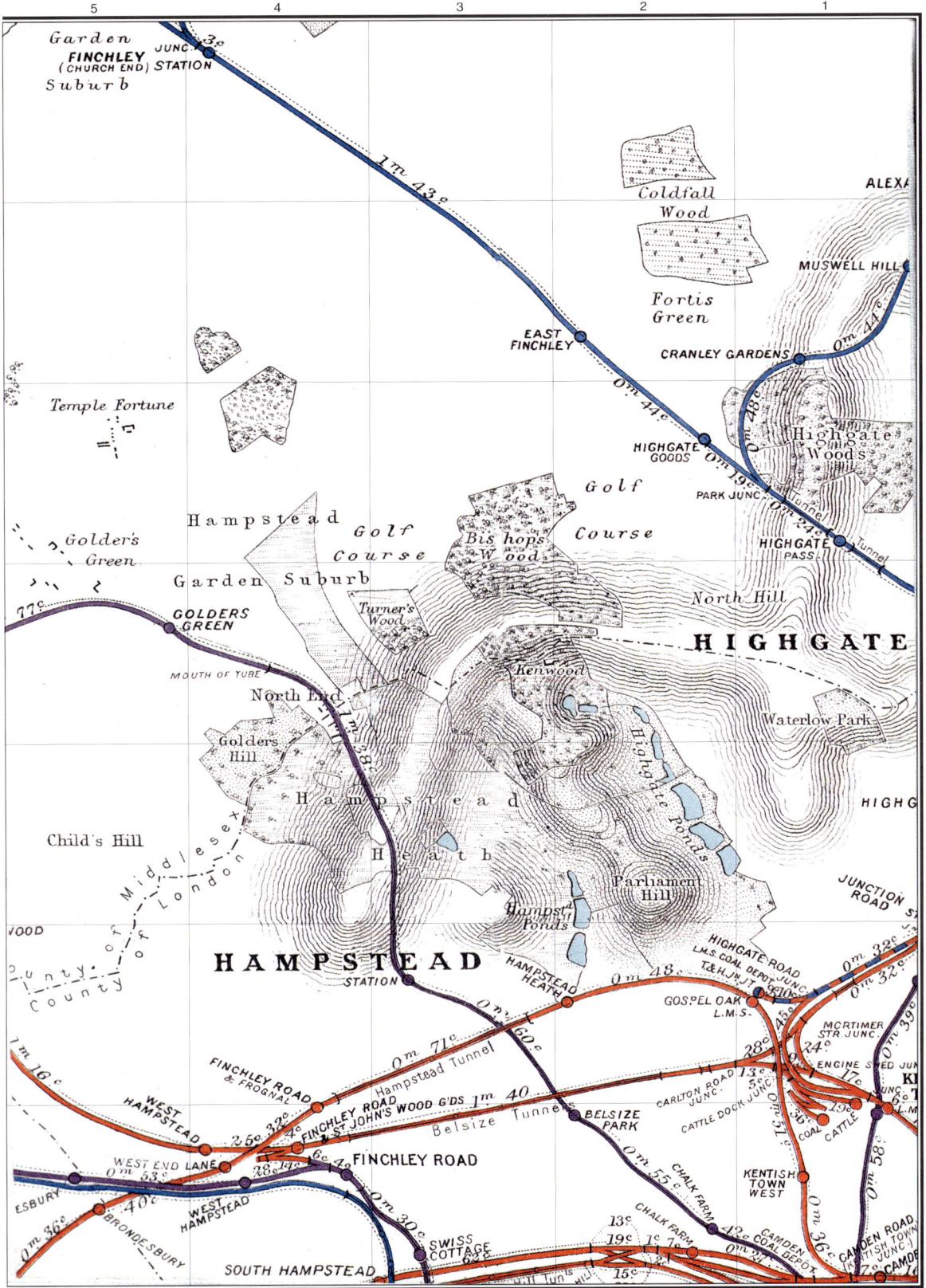

Garden
FINCHLEY (CHURCH END) STATION   JUNC.
Suburb

A

Coldfall
Wood

ALEXA

Fortis
Green

MUSWELL HILL

B

1m 43c

EAST
FINCHLEY

CRANLEY GARDENS

0m 44c

Temple Fortune

HIGHGATE
GOODS

0m 19c

Highgate
Woods

0m 48c

PARK JUNC.   0m 27c   Tunnel

C

Golf

Course

Golders
Green

Hampstead   Golf

Bishops
Wood

Course

HIGHGATE
PASS   Tunnel

Garden   Suburb

GOLDERS
GREEN

Turner's
Wood

North Hill

HIGHGATE

MOUTH OF TUBE

Kenwood

D

North End   1m 38c

Waterlow Park

Golders
Hill

Hampstead

Highgate Ponds

HIGHG

E

Child's Hill

Heath

Parliament
Hill

JUNCTION
ROAD S

Hampd
Ponds

HIGHGATE
ROAD
LMS COAL DEPOT.
T.& H. JN.JT.   9310c

0m 33c

HAMPSTEAD

STATION

HAMPSTEAD
HEATH

0m 48c

GOSPEL OAK
L.M.S.

T.&H.JN.JT.

0m 32c

MORTIMER
STR. JUNC.

F

0m 71c

0m 60c

28c   24c

ENGINE SHED JUN

0m 39c

1m 16c

FINCHLEY ROAD
& FROGNAL

Hampstead Tunnel

CARLTON ROAD
JUNC.   13c
3c

17c

JUNC.
T

WEST
HAMPSTEAD

25c 32c

FINCHLEY ROAD
ST. JOHN'S WOOD G'DS   1m 40

Belsize Tunnel

BELSIZE
PARK

CATTLE DOCK JUNC.

COAL   CATTLE

19c
36c   COAL

L.M.

WEST END LANE   0m 53c

8c 40c

FINCHLEY ROAD

0m 55c

KENTISH
TOWN
WEST

0m 58c

G

ESBURY   0m 40c

28c 47c

0m 30c

SWISS
COTTAGE

13c

CHALK FARM

19c 1c 7c

42c

CAMDEN
COAL DEPOT

0m 36c

CAMDEN ROAD
JUNC.

CAMDE

BRONDESBURY

WEST
HAMPSTEAD

0m 36c

SOUTH HAMPSTEAD

62c

CHALK FARM

15c

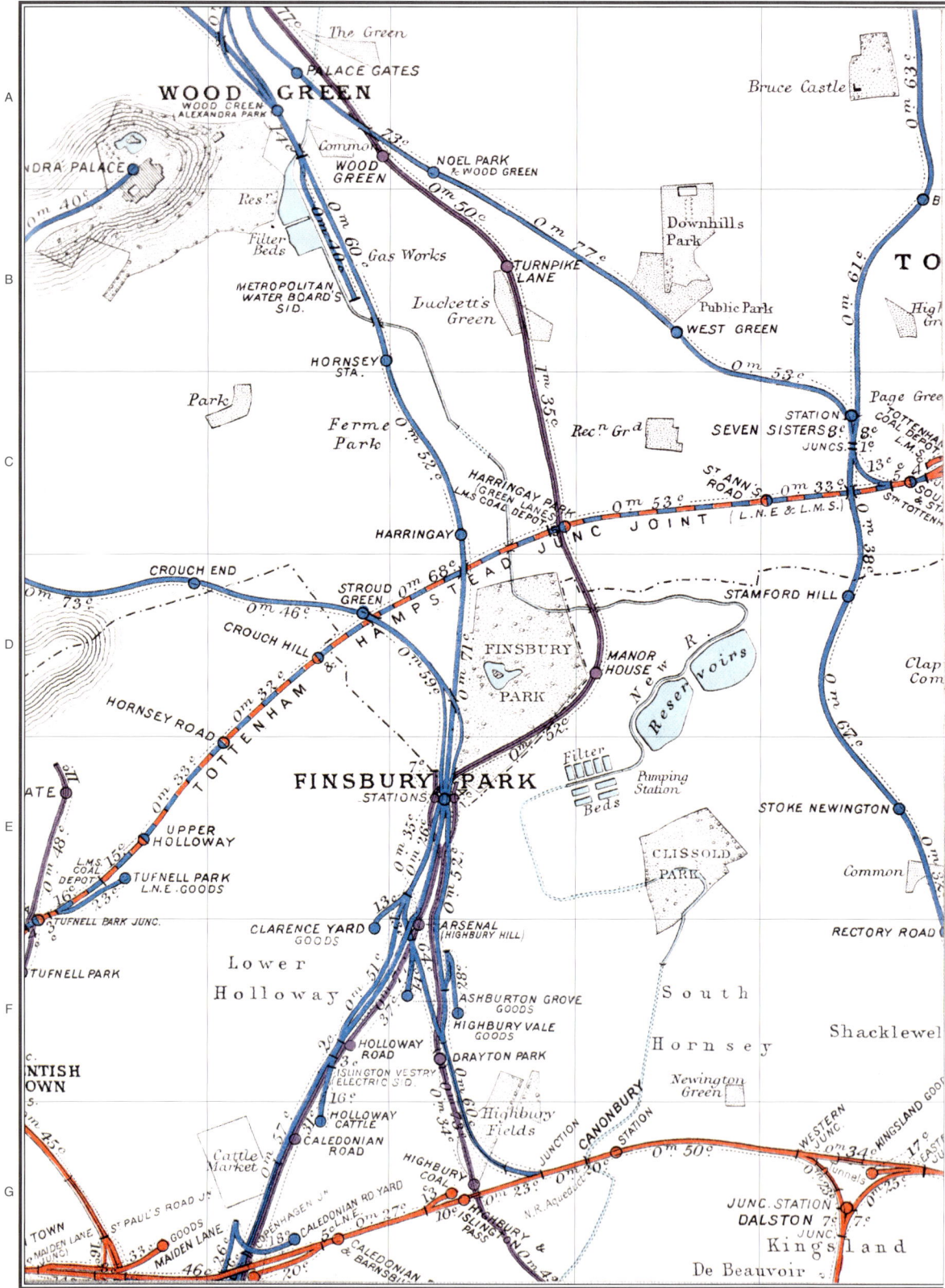

1   2   3   4   5

WOOD GREEN

PALACE GATES

Bruce Castle

WOOD GREEN
ALEXANDRA PARK

The Green

Common
WOOD
GREEN

NOEL PARK
& WOOD GREEN

Downhills
Park

Public Park

TO

ALEXANDRA PALACE

Res.ⁿ

Filter
Beds

Gas Works

TURNPIKE
LANE

Luckett's
Green

WEST GREEN

High
Gr.

METROPOLITAN
WATER BOARD'S
SID.

Park

HORNSEY
STA.

Ferme
Park

Rec.ⁿ Gr.d

Page Green

SEVEN SISTERS &.
JUNCS.

STATION

Tottenham
Coal Depot
L.M.S.

Harringay Park
(Green Lanes)
L.M.S. COAL DEPOT.

St ANN'S
ROAD

St ANN'S
ROAD

So
Sta
S. Totten

HARRINGAY

HAMPSTEAD JUNC. JOINT   (L.N.E & L.M.S.)

CROUCH END

STROUD
GREEN

STAMFORD HILL

CROUCH HILL

FINSBURY
PARK

MANOR
HOUSE

New R.

Reservoirs

Clap
Com

HORNSEY ROAD

TOTTENHAM &

Filter
Beds

Pumping
Station

FINSBURY PARK
STATIONS.

STOKE NEWINGTON

GATE

UPPER
HOLLOWAY

L.M.S.
COAL
DEPOT

TUFNELL PARK
L.N.E .GOODS

CLARENCE YARD
GOODS

ARSENAL
(HIGHBURY HILL)

CLISSOLD
PARK

Common

RECTORY ROAD

TUFNELL PARK JUNC.

TUFNELL PARK

Lower
Holloway

ASHBURTON GROVE
GOODS

HIGHBURY VALE
GOODS

DRAYTON PARK

South

Shacklewel

Hornsey

NTISH
OWN

HOLLOWAY
ROAD

ISLINGTON VESTRY
(ELECTRIC SID.)

HOLLOWAY
CATTLE

CALEDONIAN
ROAD

Cattle
Market

Highbury
Fields

Newington
Green

CANONBURY
STATION

JUNCTION

WESTERN
JUNC.

KINGSLAND GOOD

EAST
JUN

St PAUL'S ROAD J.ⁿ

HIGHBURY
COAL

HIGHBURY &
PASSAGE

N.R. AQUEDUCT

JUNC. STATION
DALSTON

JUNC.

Kingsland

TOWN
MAIDEN LANE
JUNC.

MAIDEN LANE
GOODS

COPENHAGEN J.ⁿ

CALEDONIAN RD YARD
L.N.E.

CALEDONIAN
& BARNSBU

De Beauvoir

5 4 3 2 1

A

NORTHUMBERLAND
PARK

0ᵐ 73ᶜ

Lock

1ᵐ 46ᶜ

Rᵉⁿ Grᵈ

Chapel
End

BRUCE GROVE

Higham Hill

Lloyd's
Park

B

TTENHAM

Lock

STATION

n Grᵉss
een

0ᵐ 24ᶜ

NORTH JⁿN.

0ᵐ 49ᶜ

BLACKHORSE
ROAD

METROPOLITAN WATER BOARD
SIDᵍ

0ᵐ 61ᶜ

WOOD
STREET

Recⁿ Grᵈ

0ᵐ 68ᶜ

HOE STREET

Whips Cross

0ᵐ 68ᶜ

0ᵐ 43ᶜ

13ᶜ

WEST Jⁿ

0ᵐ 13ᶜ

SOUTH JⁿN.

Recⁿ
Grᵈ

ST. JAMES
STREET

0ᵐ 12ᶜ

PASS.

WALTHAMSTOW

C

43ᶜ
8ᶜ

21

TH
ORD HILL
AM J.

OTTENHAM

0ᵐ 46ᴿ

0ᵐ 58ᶜ

Recreation
Ground

0ᵐ 27ᶜ

QUEEN'S ROAD
GOODS

Knotts
Green

COPPER MILL
JUNC.

e a

ton
mon

Springfield
Park

CLAPTON
JUNC.

5ᶜ 23ᶜ

0ᵐ 34ᶜ

0ᵐ 52ᶜ

HALL FARM
JUNC.

0ᵐ 56ᶜ

Leyton Green

0ᵐ 63ᶜ

LEYTON

D

Upper
Clapton

CLAPTON
GOODS

0ᵐ 17ᶜ

14ᶜ

County

of

County

JUNCTION

LEA BRIDGE
STATION

7ᶜ

Leyton

Marsh

0ᵐ 67ᶜ

CLAPTON
PASS.

London

of

Essex

E

North
Mill Fields

Sᵗʰ Mill
Fields

TEMPLE MILLS
SIDINGS

1ᵐ

LEYTON

0ᵐ 59ᶜ

0ᵐ 73ᶜ

Lower
Clapton

Hackney

0ᵐ 68ᶜ

0ᵐ 36ᶜ

Recreation
Ground

F

Hackney
Downs

Tunnel

Marsh

LOUGHTON JUNC.

0ᵐ 18ᶜ

CHOBHAM FᵃR.
JUNC.

1

JUNC.

HACKNEY
DOWNS

PASS.

River

0ᵐ 39ᶜ

0ᵐ 22ᶜ

G

L.N.E.
GOODS

INTERCHANGE
FOOTWAY

14ᶜ

STATION
PASS.

0ᵐ 19ᶜ

HACKNEY

COAL DEPÔT

8ᶜ

0ᵐ 29ᶜ

HOMERTON

0ᵐ 37ᶜ

HACKNEY WICK
GOODS & COAL
(L.N.E.)

VICTORIA PARK OR
HACKNEY WICK JUNC.

VICTORIA PARK
STA.

0ᵐ 46ᶜ

STRAT

CENTRAL STA.
(MAIN LINE)

9ᶜ

EASTERN

0ᵐ 28ᶜ

0ᵐ 42ᶜ

South
Hackney

Hackney

0ᵐ 6ᶜ

10ᶜ

10ᶜ

0ᵐ 6ᶜ

15ᶜ

10ᶜ

CENTRAL JUN

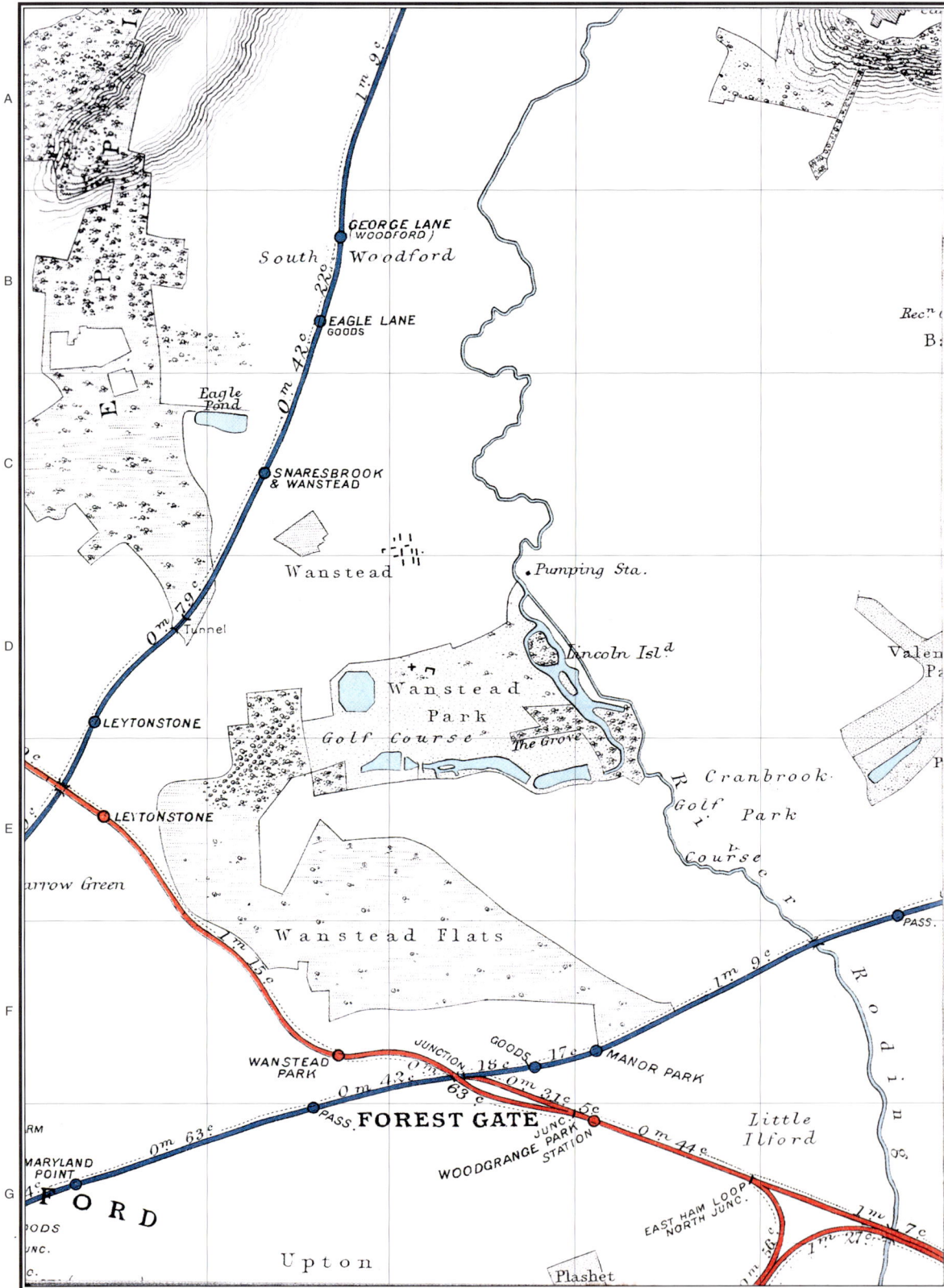

1   2   3   4   5

A

B

GEORGE LANE
(WOODFORD)

South Woodford

EAGLE LANE
GOODS

Eagle Pond

E P P I

E

Recⁿ
B:

C

SNARESBROOK
& WANSTEAD

Wanstead

Pumping Sta.

D

0 m 79 c   Tunnel

Wanstead Park

Lincoln Isl^d

Golf Course

The Grove

Val
Pa

Cranbrook

Golf Park

LEYTONSTONE

0 m 42 c

1 m 9 c

22 c

E

LEYTONSTONE

arrow Green

Course

R

Wanstead Flats

PASS.

1 m 9 c

F

1 m 15 c

WANSTEAD
PARK

JUNCTION   GOODS   18 c   17 c   MANOR PARK

0 m 43 c   63 c   0 m 31 c   5 c

Roding

G

MARYLAND
POINT

0 m 63 c   PASS.

FOREST GATE

WOODGRANGE
PARK STATION

JUNC.

0 m 44 c

Little Ilford

EAST HAM LOOP
NORTH JUNC.

1 m 7 c

1 m 2 c

F O R D

GOODS

UNC.

Upton

Plashet

1 m 36 c

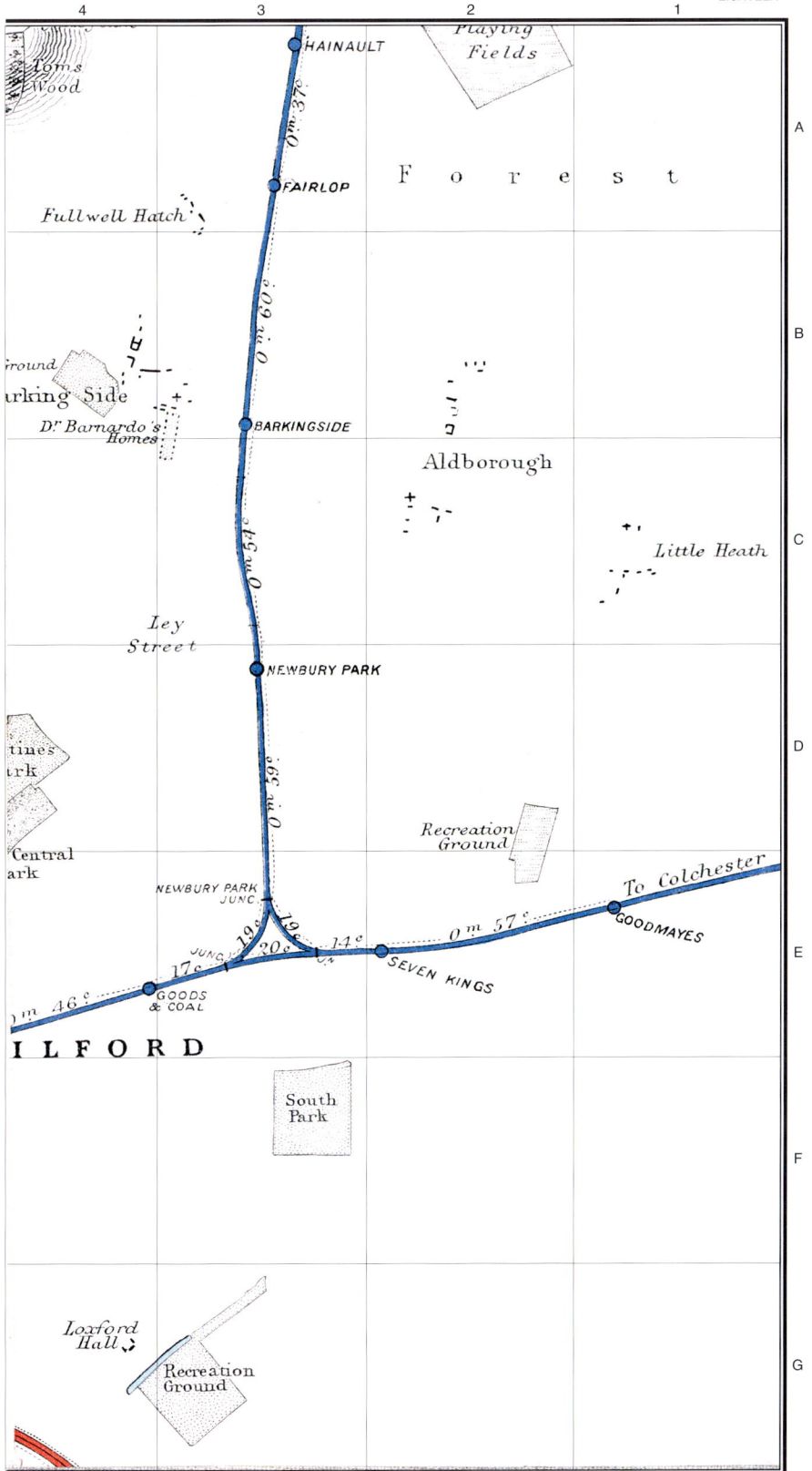

4 3 2 1

A

B

C

D

E

F

G

HAINAULT

Toms Wood

Playing Fields

0m 37c

FAIRLOP

Fullwell Hatch

F o r e s t

0 m 60c

Ground
rking Side

D.r Barnardo's Homes

BARKINGSIDE

Aldborough

Little Heath

0 m 45c

Ley Street

NEWBURY PARK

0 m 39c

tines rk

Central ark

Recreation Ground

To Colchester

NEWBURY PARK JUNC.

0m 57c

GOODMAYES

19c
JUNC 20c
17c 14c
SEVEN KINGS

0 m 46c

GOODS & COAL

I L F O R D

South Park

Loxford Hall

Recreation Ground

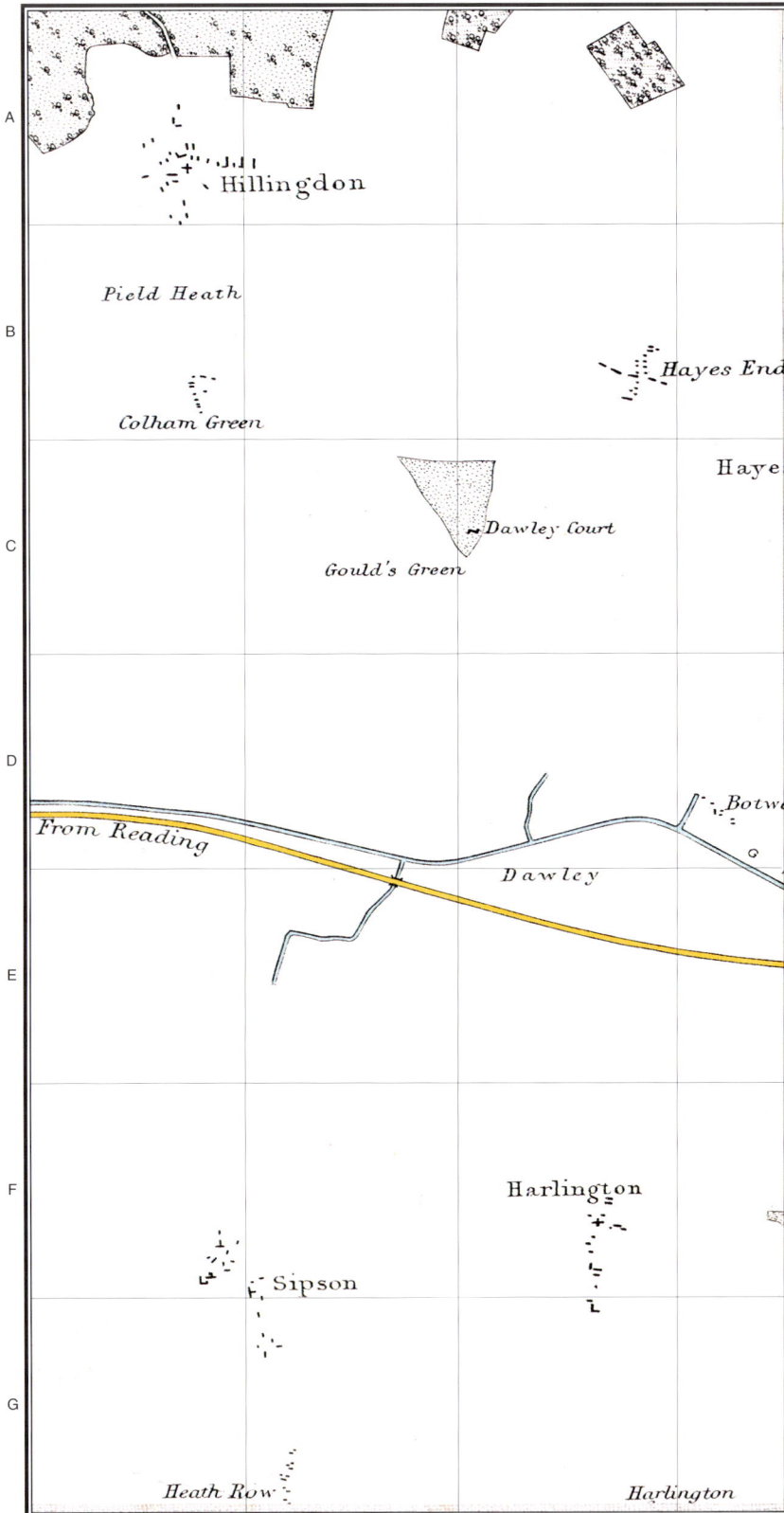

1   2   3   4

A

Hillingdon

Pield Heath

B

Hayes End

Colham Green

Haye

Dawley Court

C

Gould's Green

D

From Reading

Botw

Dawley

E

F

Harlington

Sipson

G

Heath Row

Harlington

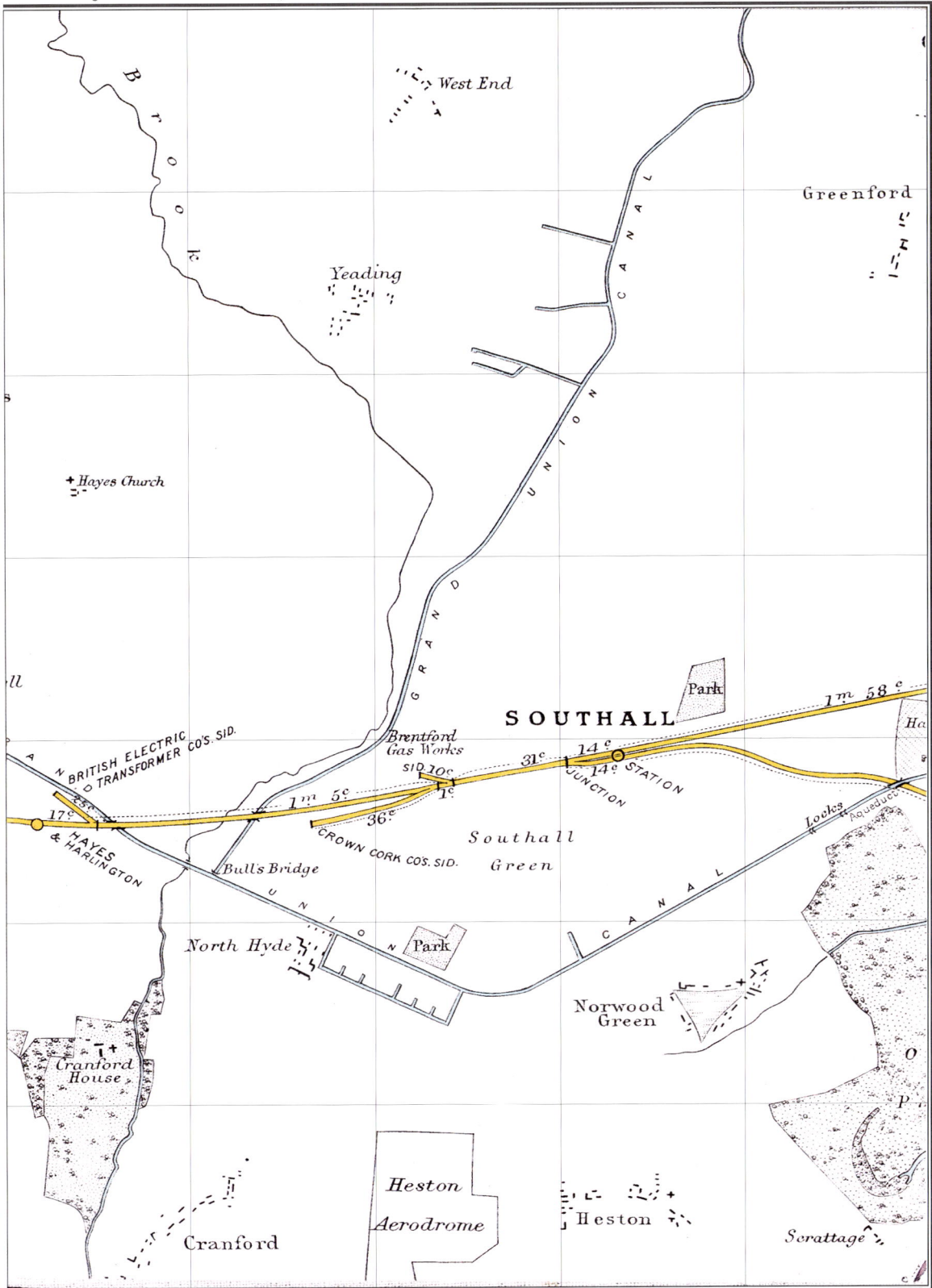

5 4 3 2 1

A

West End

Greenford

B

Yeading

C

Hayes Church

D

Park

SOUTHALL

1ᵐ 58ᶜ

*Brentford
Gas Works*
SID. 10ᶜ

31ᶜ

14ᶜ
14ᶜ

STATION

Ha

JUNCTION

BRITISH ELECTRIC
TRANSFORMER CO'S. SID.

1ᵐ 5ᶜ

1ᶜ

Locks

Aqueduct

E

25ᶜ

36ᶜ

17ᶜ

HAYES
& HARLINGTON

CROWN CORK CO'S. SID.

*Southall
Green*

CANAL

Bull's Bridge

North Hyde

Park

*Norwood
Green*

F

O

*Cranford
House*

P

*Heston
Aerodrome*

Heston

G

Cranford

Scrattage

1 2 3 4 5

GREENFORD

ALPERTON

Perivale Wood

0m 34c

0m 33c

26c EAST JUNC. 0m 30c

SOUTH JUNC.

PERIVALE HALT

SOUTH GREENFORD HALT

SANDERSON & SON'S SID.

0m 54c

40c

Brent Via

CANAL

R i v e r

Aqu

20c

Perivale

Golf

0m 61c

Viaduct

Course

Viaduct

1m 18

Viaduct

30c

BRENTHAM
(for NORTH EALING)
PLATFORM

PARK ROYAL WEST HALT

39c

PARK ROYAL

Hanger Hill

0m 54c

A

B

CASTLEBAR PARK HALT

0m 37c

Castlebar
Hill

NORTH EALING

C

R i v e r

DRAYTON GREEN HALT

JUNC.

0m 26c 0m 28c

Recr'n Ground

EALING

BROADWAY

20c

43c

HANGER LANE JN.

0m 60c

G.W. 11c 6c

0m 68c

0m 31c

STA. 6c JUNC.

0m 36c 0m 44c

JUNC. 16c WEST EALING STA.

0m 64c

Ealing Dean

Ealing Common

EALING COMMON

D

HANWELL & ELTHORNE

Viaduct

nwell Asylum

Locks

B r e n t

Walpole Park

Lammas
Park

1m 29c

1m 21c

NORTH JUNC.

ACTON TOWN

E

2m 38c

NORTHFIELDS

0m 20c

0m 20c

SOUTH EALING

Gunnersbury
Park

Little Ealing

0m 50c

Osterley Lock

BOSTON MANOR

KEW
BRIDGE

F

sterley

Viaduct

12c

Wyke Green

12c 10c

MACFARLANE'S SID.

5c

Lock

BRENTFORD TOWN GOODS

3c

GOODS

OLD KEW JUNCTION

KEW COAL

0m 28c

27c

KEW EAST

PASS. STATION

0m 29c

0m 33c

DOREY'S SID.

23c

PASS. STA.

JUNC.

Griffin Park

Kew Green

STRAND GREEN BRIDGE

FIRESTONE TYRE & RUBBER CO'S SID.

3c

SOUTHERN

BRENTFORD

0m 62c

32c

G.W.

Brentford Eyots

KEW BRIDGE

Strand on the G

OSTERLEY

G

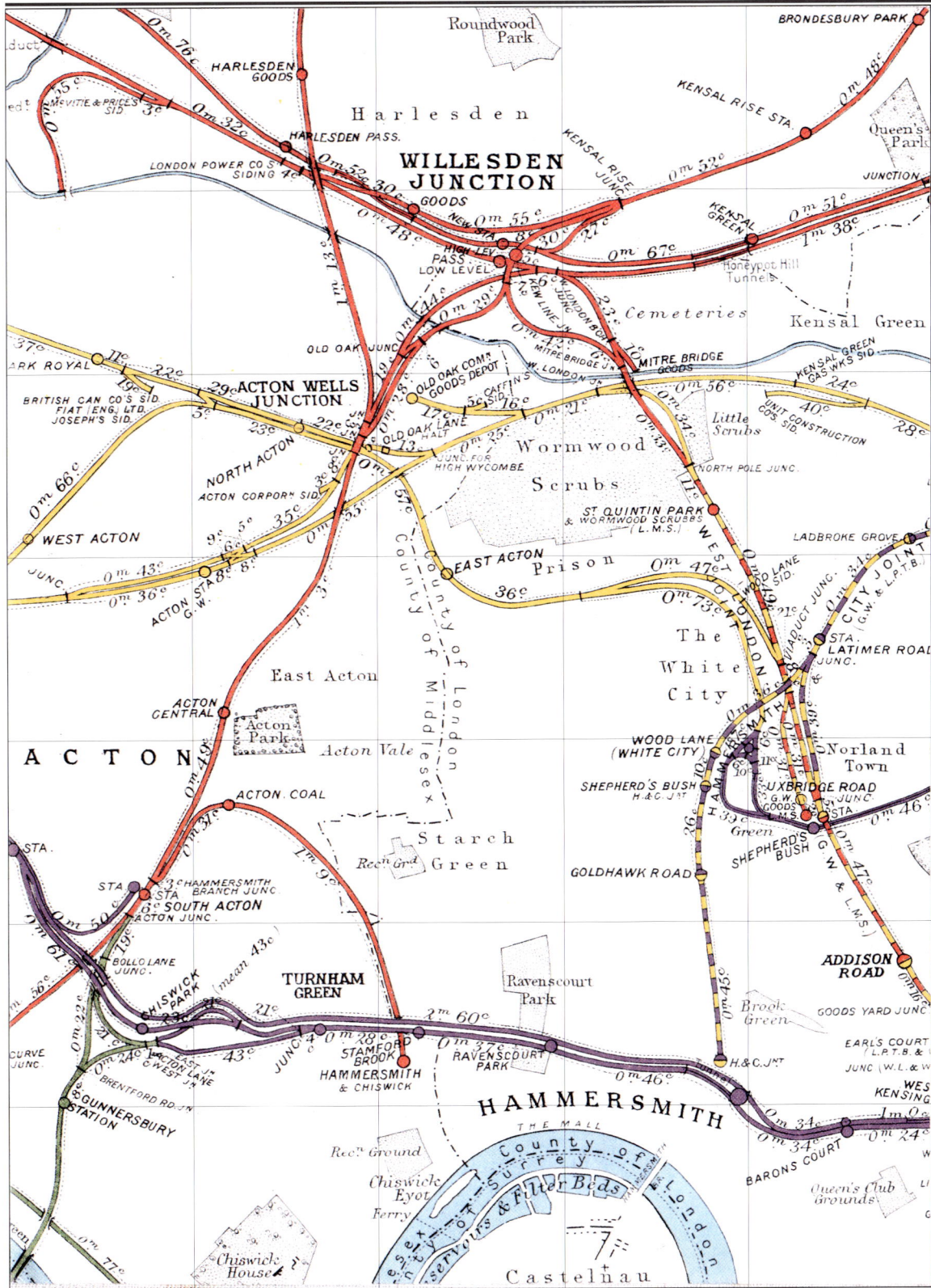

5   4   3   2   1

Roundwood Park

BRONDESBURY PARK

KENSAL RISE STA.

A

Queen's Park

duct

0 m. 76 c.

35 c.

MSVITE & PRICES SID.

0 m. 32 c.

3 c.

HARLESDEN GOODS

HARLESDEN PASS.

H a r l e s d e n

KENSAL RISE

KENSAL RISE JUNC.

0 m. 52 c.

0 m. 48 c.

JUNCTION

LONDON POWER CO'S SIDING 4 c.

0 m. 53 c.

0 m. 30 c.

WILLESDEN
JUNCTION

KENSAL GREEN

0 m. 51 c.

1 m. 38 c.

B

GOODS

NEW 0 m. 55 c.

30 c.

22 c.

0 m. 67 c.

HONEYPOT HILL TUNNELS

KENSAL GREEN GAS WKS SID.

HIGH LEVEL

LOW LEVEL

PASS

Kensal Green

NEW LINE JN.

LONDON BCH JN.

24 c.

C

0 m. 48 c.

1 44 c.

0 m. 29 c.

23 c.

MITRE BRIDGE JN.

MITRE BRIDGE GOODS

KENSAL GREEN

UNIT CONSTRUCTION CO'S SID.

OLD OAK JUNC.

OLD OAK COM.

W. LONDON JN.

0 m. 56 c.

40 c.

28 c.

37 c.

11 c.

OAK ROYAL

22 c.

ACTON WELLS
JUNCTION

19 c.

GOODS DEPOT

MITRE BRIDGE JN.

Little Scrubs

BRITISH CAN CO'S SID.
FIAT (ENG.) LTD.
JOSEPH'S SID.

29 c.

3 c.

22 c.

OLD OAK JN.

17 c.

OLD OAK LANE HALT

16 c.

CAFFIN'S

0 m. 34 c.

23 c.

13 c.

JUNC. FOR HIGH WYCOMBE

0 m. 21 c.

W o r m w o o d

NORTH POLE JUNC.

0 m. 66 c.

NORTH ACTON

0 m. 25 c.

S c r u b s

11 c.

0 m. 47 c.

LADBROKE GROVE

CITY JOINT (G.W. & L.P.T.B.)

D

ACTON CORPORN SID.

57 c.

35 c.

55 c.

St QUINTIN PARK & WORMWOOD SCRUBS (L.M.S.)

OLD LANE SID.

21 c.

VIADUCT JUNC.

STA. LATIMER ROAD

WEST ACTON

9 c.

36 c.

8 c.

8 c.

EAST ACTON

P r i s o n

0 m. 73 c.

LATIMER ROAD JUNC.

JUNC.

0 m. 43 c.

0 m. 36 c.

ACTON STA. G.W.

1 m. 7 c.

36 c.

T h e

0 m. 47 c.

W h i t e

C i t y

WOOD LANE (WHITE CITY)

Norland Town

East Acton

ACTON CENTRAL

Acton Park

Acton Vale

C o u n t y   o f   M i d d l e s e x

C o u n t y   o f   L o n d o n

SHEPHERD'S BUSH H.&C. JT

UXBRIDGE ROAD JUNC.

G.W. LMS

0 m. 46 c.

E

A C T O N

0 m. 48 c.

ACTON COAL

Green

SHEPHERD'S BUSH

STA.

1 m. 9 c.

S t a r c h

G r e e n

H.&C.J'NT

GOLDHAWK ROAD

G.W. & L.M.S.

0 m. 47 c.

STA.

STA. HAMMERSMITH BRANCH JUNC.

Rec'n Gr'd

ADDISON ROAD

F

BOLLO LANE JUNC.

0 m. 50 c.

79 c.

SOUTH ACTON

ACTON JUNC.

CHISWICK PARK

TURNHAM GREEN

Ravenscourt Park

Brook Green

GOODS YARD JUNC.

0 m. 61 c.

0 m. 22 c.

21 c.

(mean 43 c.)

21 c.

2 m. 60 c.

0 m. 45 c.

EARLS COURT (L.P.T.B. & JUNC (W.L. & W

CURVE JUNC.

21 c.

43 c.

JUNC 4

STAMFORD BROOK

0 m. 28 c.

0 m. 37 c.

RAVENSCOURT PARK

WES' KENSING

ACTON LANE G. WEST JN.

BRENTFORD RD. JN.

HAMMERSMITH & CHISWICK

0 m. 46 c.

H.&C. J'NT

BARONS COURT

0 m. 34 c.

1 m. 0

GUNNERSBURY STATION

HAMMERSMITH

0 m. 34 c.

0 m. 24 c.

Queen's Club Grounds

G

THE MALL

Rec'n Ground

C o u n t y   o f   S u r r e y

R e s e r v o i r s   &   F i l t e r   B e d s

C o u n t y   o f   L o n d o n

Chiswick Eyot

Ferry

0 m. 77 c.

Chiswick House

C a s t e l n a u

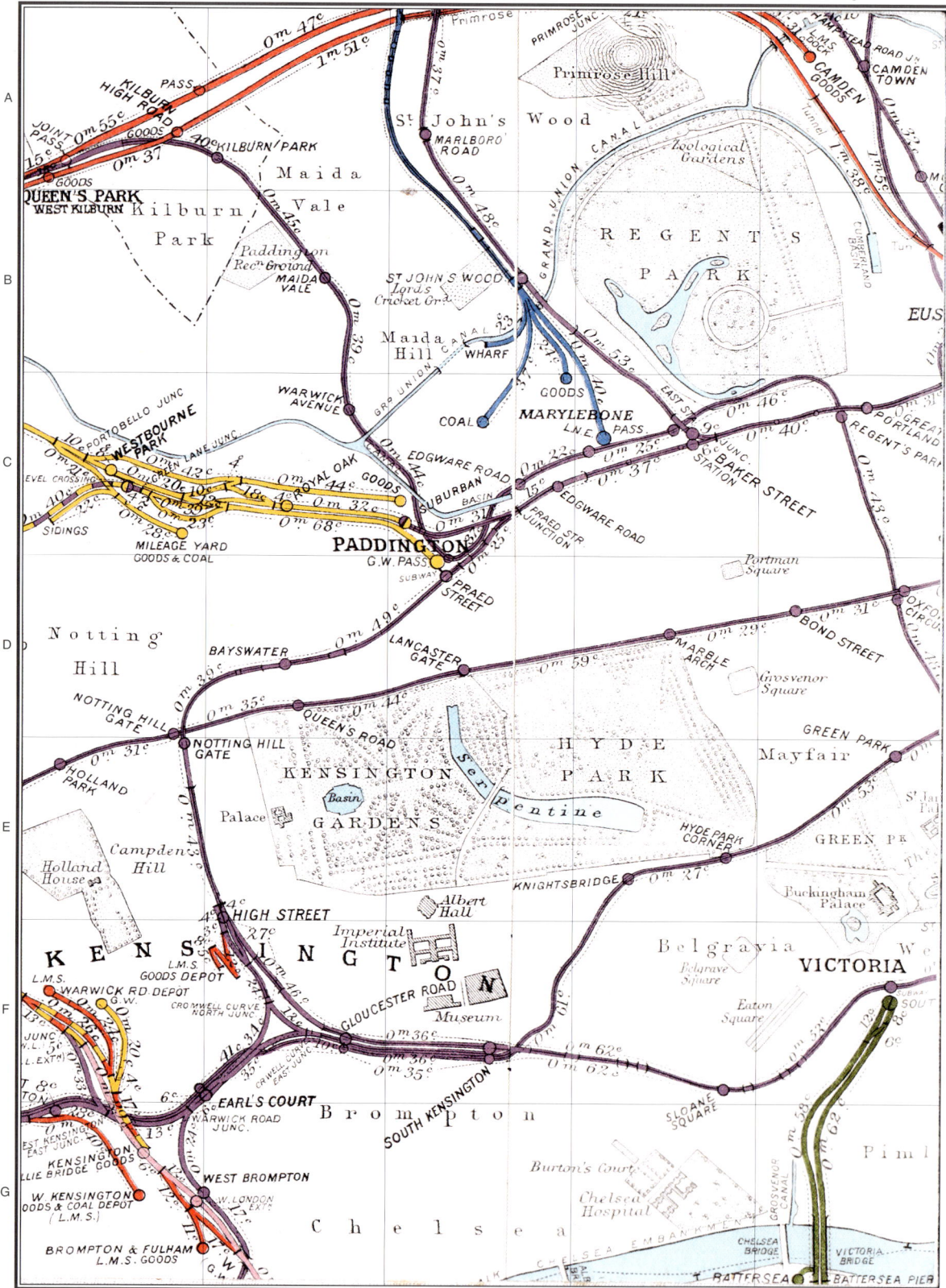

1   2   3   4   5

A

0m 47c
1m 51c
KILBURN
HIGH ROAD
PASS.
Primrose
PRIMROSE JUNC.
Primrose Hill
HAMPSTEAD ROAD Jn
CAMDEN DOCK
CAMDEN GOODS
CAMDEN TOWN
JOINT PASS.
0m 55c
GOODS
15c
0m 37
QUEEN'S PARK
WEST KILBURN
GOODS
40c KILBURN PARK
Maida Vale
St John's Wood
Zoological Gardens
GRAND UNION CANAL
CUMBERLAND BASIN
Tunnel
1m 38c
1m 51c

B

Kilburn Park
St JOHN'S ROAD
MARLBORO' ROAD
0m 48c
St JOHN'S WOOD
Lords Cricket Grd.
REGENT'S PARK
EUS
Paddington Recn Ground
MAIDA VALE
0m 36c
Maida Hill
Gro. Union Canal
WHARF
53
GOODS
EAST S.
0m 53c
0m 40
WARWICK AVENUE
COAL
MARYLEBONE
L.N.E.R.
PASS.
0m 46c
GREAT PORTLAND
REGENT'S PARK
0m 31

C

Notting Hill
PORTOBELLO JUNC
WESTBOURNE PARK
LANE JUNC.
0m 42c
4c
ROYAL OAK
14c
GOODS
0m 44c
EDGWARE ROAD
SUBURBAN
0m 22c
0m 25c
0m 37c
JUNC.
BAKER STREET STATION
0m 40c
0m 43c
LEVEL CROSSING
0m 40c
20c 10c
18c
16c
0m 33c
0m 31
15c
EDGWARE ROAD
SIDINGS
0m 28c
23c
0m 68c
MILEAGE YARD
GOODS & COAL
PADDINGTON
G.W. PASS.
SUBWAY
0m 25c
FRAED STR. JUNCTION
FRAED STREET

D

Notting Hill
BAYSWATER
0m 49c
LANCASTER GATE
PRAED STREET
MARBLE ARCH
0m 29c
BOND STREET
0m 31
OXFORD CIRCUS
0m 26c
0m 35c
QUEEN'S ROAD
0m 41c
0m 59c
Grosvenor Square
Portman Square
NOTTING HILL GATE
0m 31c
NOTTING HILL GATE
KENSINGTON GARDENS
Serpentine
HYDE PARK
GREEN PARK
HOLLAND PARK
Palace
Basin
Mayfair

E

Holland House
Campden Hill
GARDENS
Albert Hall
KNIGHTSBRIDGE
HYDE PARK CORNER
0m 27c
GREEN PK
Buckingham Palace
St Ja
The

F

KENSINGTON
4c
HIGH STREET
Imperial Institute
Belgravia
VICTORIA
L.M.S.
GOODS DEPOT
L.M.S.
Museum
SUBWAY
SOUT
6c
WARWICK RD. DEPOT
G.W.
CROMWELL CURVE NORTH JUNC.
0m 46c
GLOUCESTER ROAD
0m 36c
0m 62c
Belgrave Square
0m 62c
Eaton Square
6c
JUNC.
N.L.
L.EXTN.
0m 34c
0m 35c
CRWELL CURVE EAST JUNC.
0m 62c
SLOANE SQUARE
GROSVENOR CANAL
8 & c
6c
13c
EARL'S COURT
WARWICK ROAD JUNC.
SOUTH KENSINGTON
0m 62c
Pim l

G

W. KENSINGTON GOODS & COAL DEPOT (L.M.S.)
KENSINGTON GOODS
LLIE BRIDGE
WEST BROMPTON
W. LONDON EXTN.
Brompton
Burton's Court
Chelsea Hospital
CHELSEA EMBANKMEN
CHELSEA BRIDGE
VICTORIA BRIDGE
BATTERSEA
BATTERSEA PIER
BROMPTON & FULHAM
L.M.S. GOODS
Chelsea

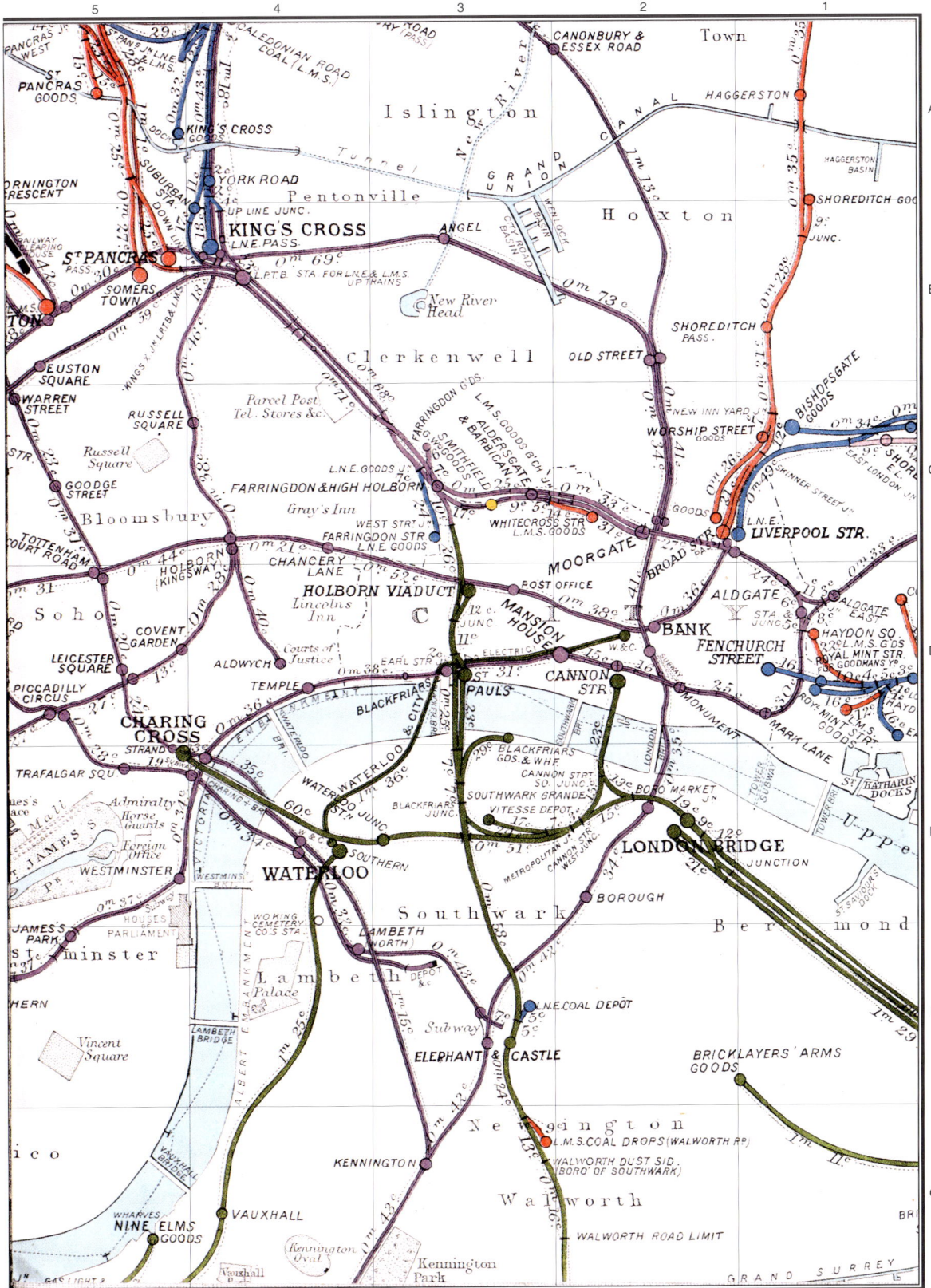

5 4 3 2 1

A

B

C

D

E

F

G

ST PANCRAS GOODS
ST PANCRAS
KING'S CROSS
KING'S CROSS GOODS
YORK ROAD
KING'S CROSS L.N.E. PASS.
SOMERS TOWN
MORNINGTON CRESCENT
EUSTON SQUARE
WARREN STREET
RUSSELL SQUARE
GOODGE STREET
Bloomsbury
TOTTENHAM COURT ROAD
Soho
HOLBORN (KINGSWAY)
CHANCERY LANE
FARRINGDON & HIGH HOLBORN
FARRINGDON STR.
L.N.E. GOODS
HOLBORN VIADUCT
COVENT GARDEN
LEICESTER SQUARE
PICCADILLY CIRCUS
ALDWYCH
TEMPLE
CHARING CROSS
TRAFALGAR SQU.
WESTMINSTER
ST JAMES'S PARK
HOUSES OF PARLIAMENT
LAMBETH (NORTH)
WATERLOO
Lambeth Palace
Vincent Square
LAMBETH BRIDGE
VAUXHALL BRIDGE
NINE ELMS GOODS
VAUXHALL
KENNINGTON
Kennington Oval
Kennington Park
Islington
Pentonville
ANGEL
Clerkenwell
New River Head
Hoxton
HAGGERSTON
HAGGERSTON BASIN
SHOREDITCH GOODS
SHOREDITCH PASS.
OLD STREET
WORSHIP STREET
BISHOPSGATE GOODS
LIVERPOOL STR.
MOORGATE
ALDGATE
BANK
FENCHURCH STREET
HAYDON SQ.
MANSION HOUSE
POST OFFICE
BROAD STR.
MARK LANE
CANNON STR.
MONUMENT
ST PAULS
BLACKFRIARS
WHITECROSS STR. L.M.S. GOODS
SMITHFIELD & WESTN. GOODS
ALDERSGATE & BARBICAN
FARRINGDON GDS.
WATERLOO JUNC.
BLACKFRIARS JUNC.
SOUTHWARK
Bermondsey
LONDON BRIDGE
BOROUGH
BLACKFRIARS GDS. & WHF.
CANNON STR. SO. JUNC.
SOUTHWARK GRANDE VITESSE DEPOT
BORO MARKET JUNC.
TOWER SUBWAY
ST KATHARINE DOCKS
Upper
BRICKLAYERS' ARMS GOODS
L.N.E. COAL DEPÔT
ELEPHANT & CASTLE
Newington
L.M.S. COAL DROPS (WALWORTH RD.)
WALWORTH DUST SID. (BORO' OF SOUTHWARK)
Walworth
WALWORTH ROAD LIMIT
GRAND SURREY
GRAND UNION CANAL
RIVER

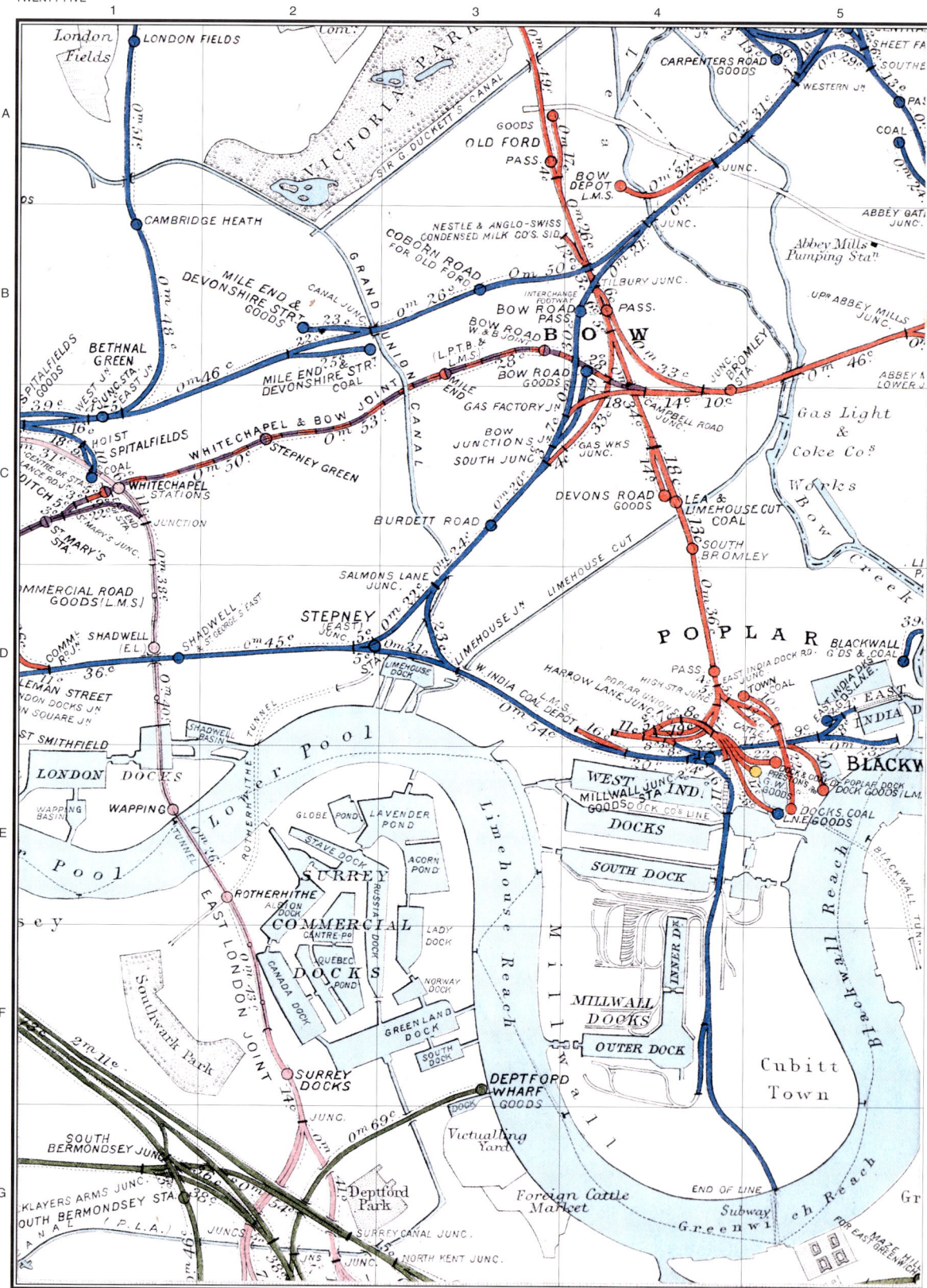

1 2 3 4 5

London Fields
LONDON FIELDS

London Fields

VICTORIA PARK

CARPENTERS ROAD GOODS
WESTERN JN.
SHEET FA
SOUTHE
COAL
PASS

CAMBRIDGE HEATH

OLD FORD
GOODS
PASS.
BOW DEPOT L.M.S.
JUNC.
JUNC.
ABBEY GATE
JUNC.
Abbey Mills Pumping Sta.n
UPR ABBEY MILLS JUNC.

SIR G. DUCKETT'S CANAL
COBURN ROAD FOR OLD FORD
NESTLE & ANGLO-SWISS CONDENSED MILK CO.S SID.
TILBURY JUNC.
PASS.
BOW ROAD PASS.
BROMLEY

MILE END & DEVONSHIRE STR. GOODS
GRAND UNION CANAL
CANAL JUNC.
BOW ROAD (W. & G.)
BOW ROAD PASS. (L.P.T.B. & L.M.S.)
ABBEY MILLS LOWER J.

BETHNAL GREEN
SPITALFIELDS GOODS
WEST JN
JUNC. STA
EAST JN
MILE END & DEVONSHIRE STR. COAL
MILE END
BOW ROAD GOODS
GAS FACTORY JN.
JUNC.
Gas Light & Coke Co.s

HOIST
SPITALFIELDS
WHITECHAPEL & BOW JOINT
STEPNEY GREEN
BOW JUNCTIONS SOUTH JUNC.
GAS WKS JUNC.
Works
Bow Creek

CENTRE OF STA
COMM. RD JN
WHITECHAPEL STATIONS
DITCH
ST. MARY'S JN.
END
JUNCTION
BURDETT ROAD
DEVONS ROAD GOODS
LEA & LIMEHOUSE CUT COAL
SOUTH BROMLEY

ST. MARY'S STA.
COMMERCIAL ROAD GOODS (L.M.S.)
SALMONS LANE JUNC.
LIMEHOUSE CUT
LIMEHOUSE JN.
POPLAR

SHADWELL (E.L.)
COMM. RD JN
SHADWELL ST. GEORGE'S EAST
STEPNEY EAST JUNC.
LIMEHOUSE JUNC.
BLACKWALL G.DS & COAL
PASS.
EAST INDIA DOCK RD
EAST INDIA DKS

COLEMAN STREET
LONDON DOCKS JN
SQUARE JN.
SHADWELL STA.
LIMEHOUSE DOCK
L.W. INDIA DOCK STA.
HARROW LANE JUNC.
HIGH STR. JUNC.
POPLAR UNION JN.
EAST INDIA DK JUNC.
TOWN
L.M.S.
GDS JN.
EAST INDIA

ST. SMITHFIELD
SHADWELL BASIN
ROTHERHITHE TUNNEL
Lower Pool
L.W. INDIA COAL DEPOT
WEST MILLWALL GOODS
DOCK CO.S LINE
PRESS & COAL G.W.
POPLAR DOCK G.W. GOODS
POPLAR DOCK GOODS L.M.
BLACKW

LONDON DOCKS
WAPPING BASIN
WAPPING
GLOBE POND
LAVENDER POND
STAVE DOCK
ACORN POND
WEST INDIA
DOCKS
SOUTH DOCK
DOCKS COAL
L.N.E. GOODS

Pool
Pool
EAST LONDON JOINT
ROTHERHITHE
ALBION DOCK
SURREY COMMERCIAL DOCKS
CENTRE PO
RUSSIA DOCK
LADY DOCK
Limehouse Reach
INNER DK

Southwark Park
CANADA DOCK
QUEBEC POND
NORWAY DOCK
GREENLAND DOCK
SOUTH DOCK
MILLWALL DOCKS
OUTER DOCK
Millwall
Cubitt Town
Blackwall Reach

SOUTH BERMONDSEY JUNC.
SURREY DOCKS
JUNC.
DEPTFORD WHARF GOODS
Victualling Yard
Foreign Cattle Market
END OF LINE
Subway Greenwi
MAZE HILL FOR EAST GREENWICH

KLAYERS ARMS JUNC.
SOUTH BERMONDSEY STA.
CANAL (P.L.A.)
JUNCS.
JNS
JUNC.
Deptford Park
SURREY CANAL JUNC.
NORTH KENT JUNC.
Deptford Park
ch Reach
Gr

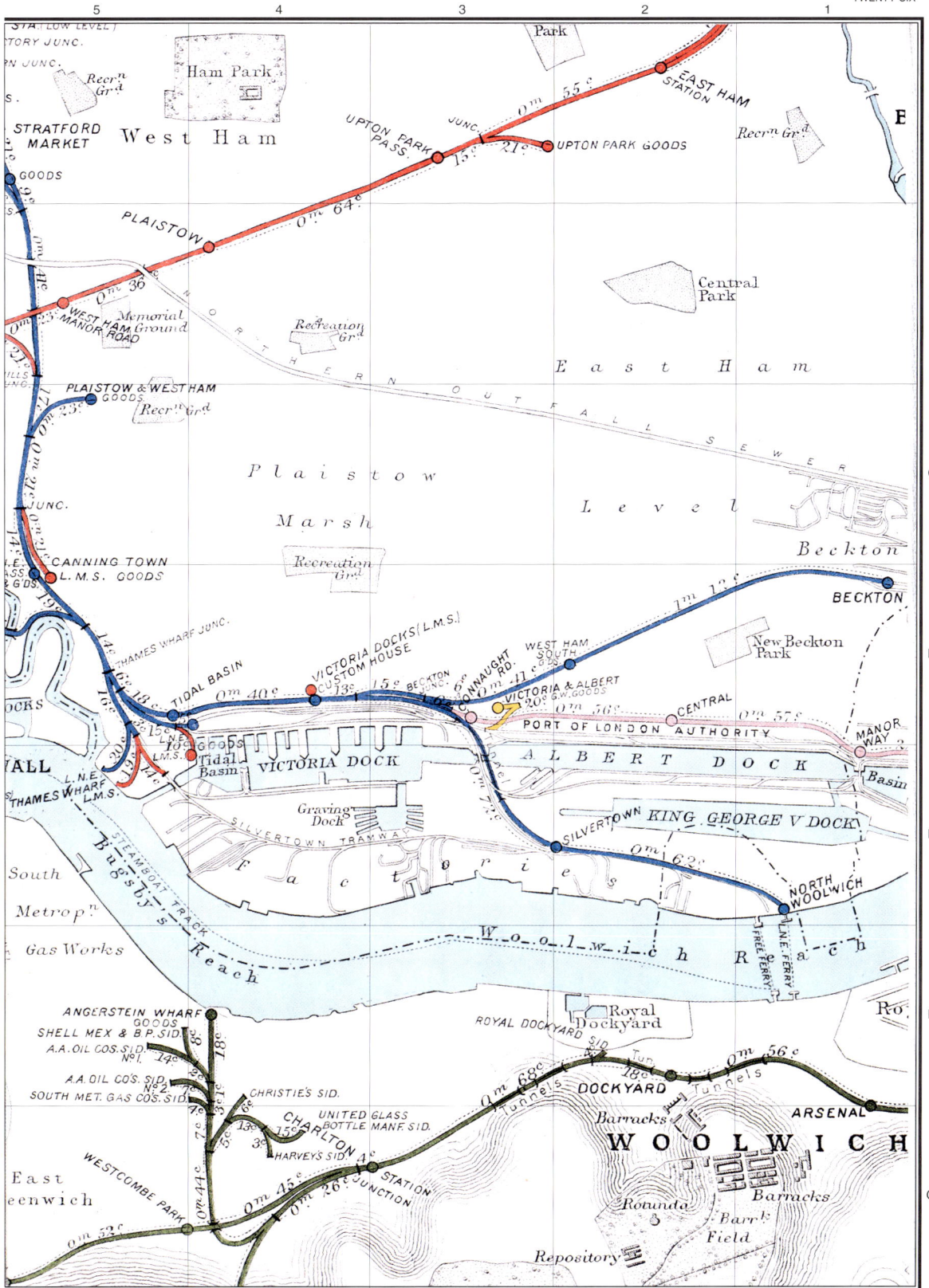

5   4   3   2   1

A

B

C

D

E

F

G

STR. (LOW LEVEL)
TORY JUNC.
N JUNC.
Recrⁿ Gr^d
Ham Park
Park
EAST HAM
STATION

STRATFORD
MARKET
West Ham
UPTON PARK
PASS.
JUNC.
0m 55c
Recrⁿ Gr^d
E

GOODS
15c
21c
UPTON PARK GOODS

PLAISTOW
0m 64c
Central
Park

0m 36c
WEST HAM
MANOR ROAD
Memorial
Ground
Recreation
Gr^d
East Ham

MILLS
NC.
PLAISTOW & WEST HAM
GOODS
Recrⁿ Gr^d
N O R T H E R N   O U T F A L L   S E W E R

23c
P l a i s t o w
L e v e l

JUNC.
M a r s h
Recreation
Gr^d
Beckton

L.E.
ASS
'DS
CANNING TOWN
L.M.S. GOODS
19c
1m 12c
BECKTON

THAMES WHARF JUNC.
14c
18c
TIDAL BASIN
Om 40c
VICTORIA DOCKS (L.M.S.)
CUSTOM HOUSE
13c
15c
BECKTON
JUNC.
CONNAUGHT
RD.
WEST HAM
SOUTH
GDS.
New Beckton
Park

16c
18c
6m 0c
VICTORIA & ALBERT
G.W. GOODS
20c
MANOR
WAY

DOCKS
L.N.E.
L.M.S. GOODS
15c
Tidal
Basin
VICTORIA DOCK
PORT OF LONDON AUTHORITY
CENTRAL
0m 57c
Basin

20c
14c

ALL
L.N.E.
THAMES WHARF
L.M.S.
Graving
Dock
SILVERTOWN TRAMWAY
A L B E R T   D O C K

South
Metropⁿ
Gas Works
B u g s b y ' s   R e a c h
F a c t o r i e s
SILVERTOWN
KING GEORGE V DOCK
0m 62c
NORTH
WOOLWICH

STEAMBOAT TRACK
W o o l w i c h   R e a c h
FREE FERRY
L.N.E. FERRY

ANGERSTEIN WHARF
GOODS
SHELL MEX & B.P. SID.
A.A. OIL COS. SID.
No 1
18c
A.A. OIL COS. SID.
No 2
SOUTH MET. GAS COS. SID.
14c
CHRISTIE'S SID.
UNITED GLASS
BOTTLE MANF. SID.
Royal
Dockyard
ROYAL DOCKYARD
SID.
Tun.
0m 68c
18c
Tunnels
0m 56c
Ro.

13c
15c
CHARLTON
HARVEY'S SID.
4c
0m 68c
Tunnels
DOCKYARD
Tunnels
ARSENAL

East
eenwich
0m 44c
WESTCOMBE PARK
0m 45c
3c
0m 26c
STATION
JUNCTION
4c
W O O L W I C H

0m 53c
Rotunda
Barracks
Barr^k
Field
Barracks

Repository

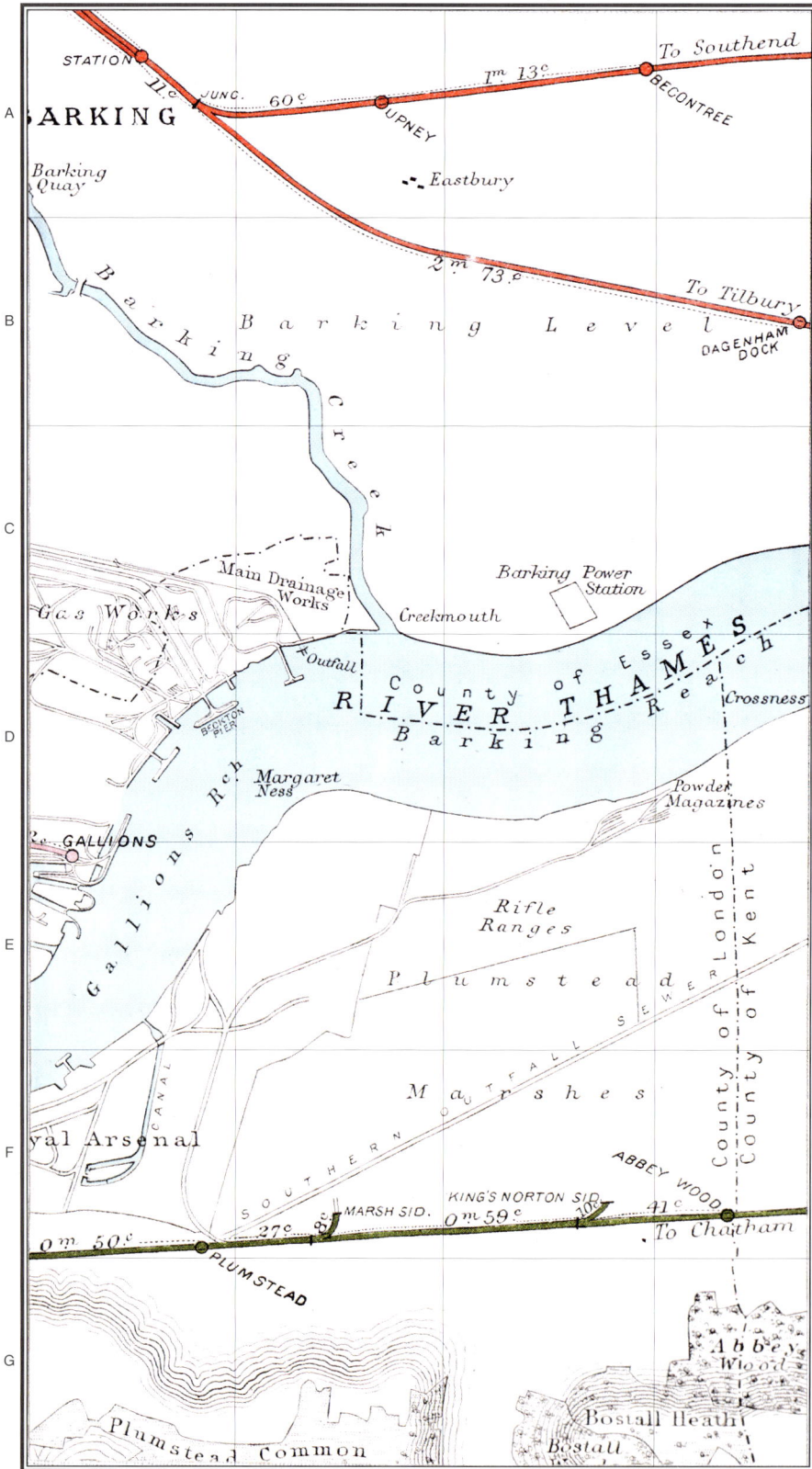

1   2   3   4

STATION

BARKING

JUNG. 11.c 60.c UPNEY 1ᵐ 13.c BECONTREE To Southend

A

Eastbury

Barking
Quay

2ᵐ 73.c To Tilbury

B Barking Creek Barking Level DAGENHAM DOCK

C Main Drainage Works Barking Power Station

Gas Works Creekmouth

Outfall

BECKTON PIER

County of Essex

D RIVER THAMES Crossness

Barking Reach

Margaret Ness

Gallions Rch.

Powder Magazines

Rch. GALLIONS

Rifle Ranges

E Gallions Reach Plumstead

County of London
County of Kent

F Marshes

CANAL

yal Arsenal

SOUTHERN OUTFALL SEWER

ABBEY WOOD

MARSH SID. KING'S NORTON SID.

27.c 8.c 0ᵐ 59.c 10.c 41.c To Chatham

0ᵐ 50.c PLUMSTEAD

G Abbey Wood

Plumstead Common Bostall Heath

Bostall

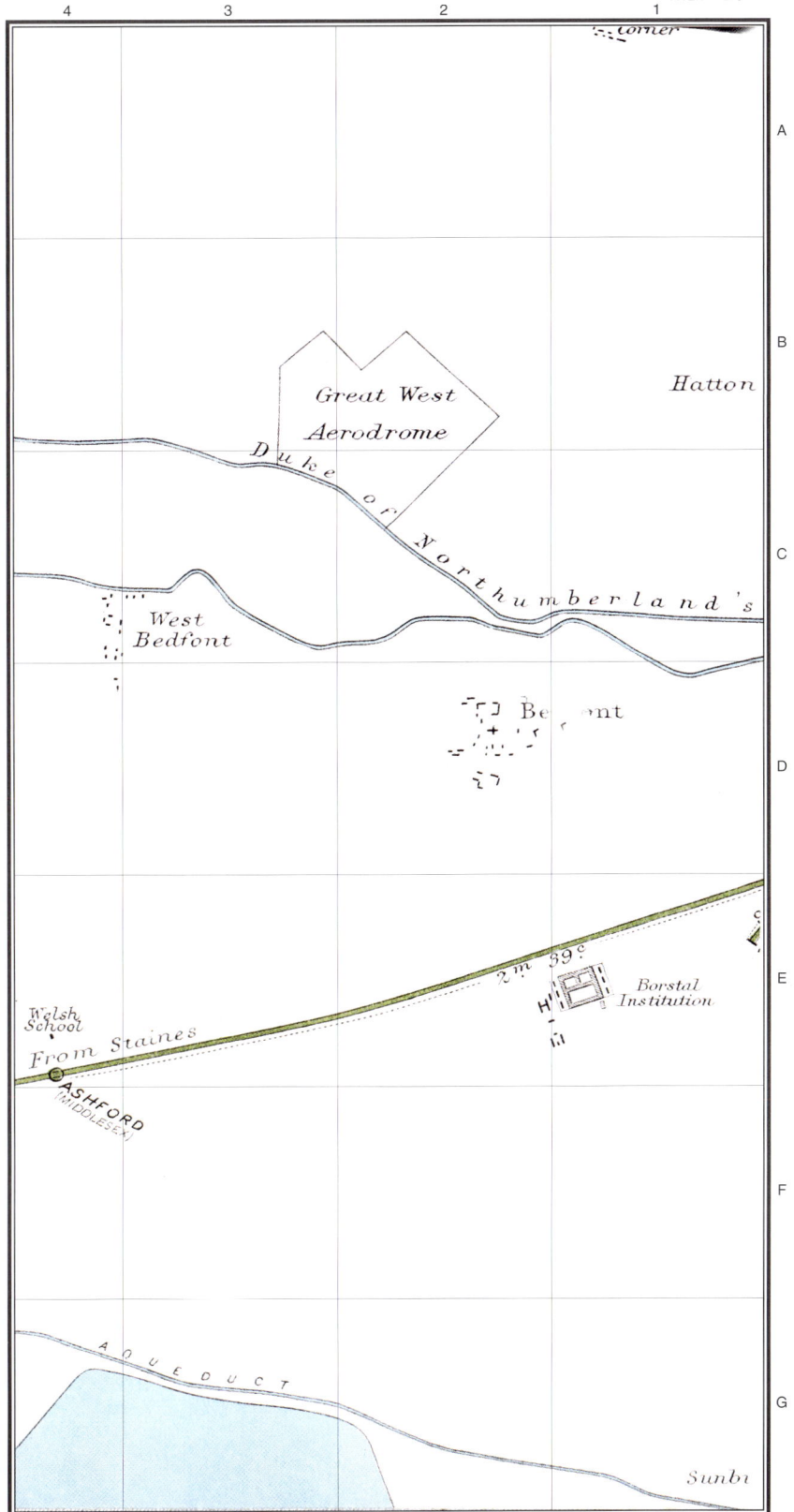

4   3   2   1

corner

A

B

Great West

Aerodrome   *Hatton*

$D u k e$ $o f$

$N o r t h u m b e r l a n d ' s$ C

West

Bedfont

Be   ont   D

2^m 39^c

Borstal

Institution   E

Welsh

School

From Staines

ASHFORD

(MIDDLESEX)   F

$A Q U E D U C T$

G

Sunbu

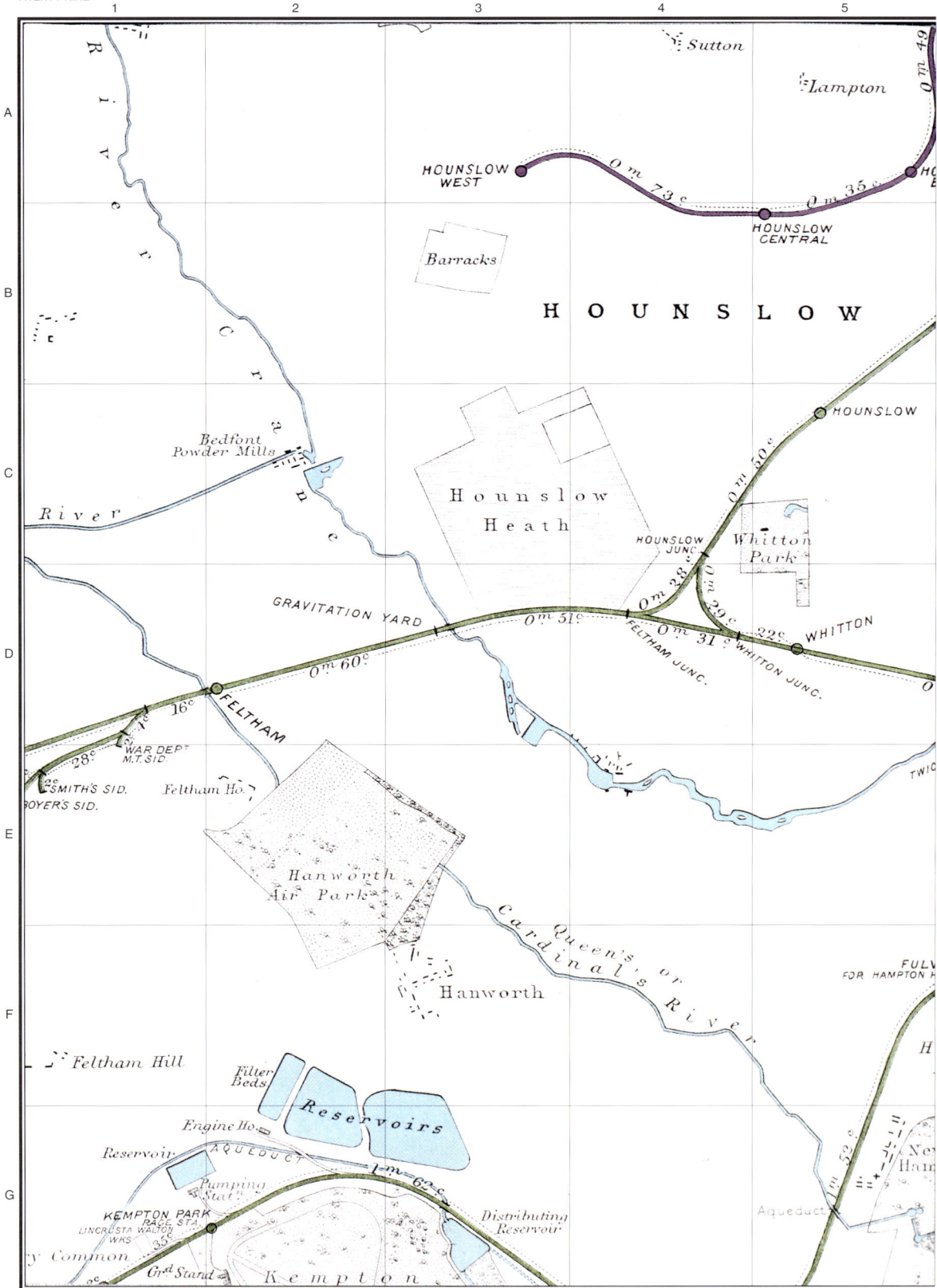

1 2 3 4 5

A

Sutton

Lampton

0 m 49

HOUNSLOW WEST

0 m 73 c

0 m 35 c

HOUNSLOW CENTRAL

HO

B

Barracks

H O U N S L O W

HOUNSLOW

C

Bedfont Powder Mills

Hounslow Heath

0 m 50 c

Whitton Park

River

HOUNSLOW JUNC.

D

GRAVITATION YARD

0 m 51 c

0 m 28 c

0 m 29 c

WHITTON

FELTHAM JUNC.

0 m 31 c

WHITTON JUNC.

22 c

0 m 60 c

16 c

FELTHAM

28 c

WAR DEPT M.T. SID.

TWI

SMITH'S SID.

BOYER'S SID.

Feltham Ho.

E

Hanworth Air Park

Queen's or Cardinal's River

FUL

FOR HAMPTON

Hanworth

F

Feltham Hill

Filter Beds

Reservoirs

0 m 52 c

Ne Han

Engine Ho.

Reservoir

AQUEDUCT

1 m 60 c

Pumping Stat.

G

KEMPTON PARK

RACE STA.

UNCRUSTA WALTON WKS

35

Distributing Reservoir

Aqueduct

y Common

Gr.d Stand

K e m p t o n

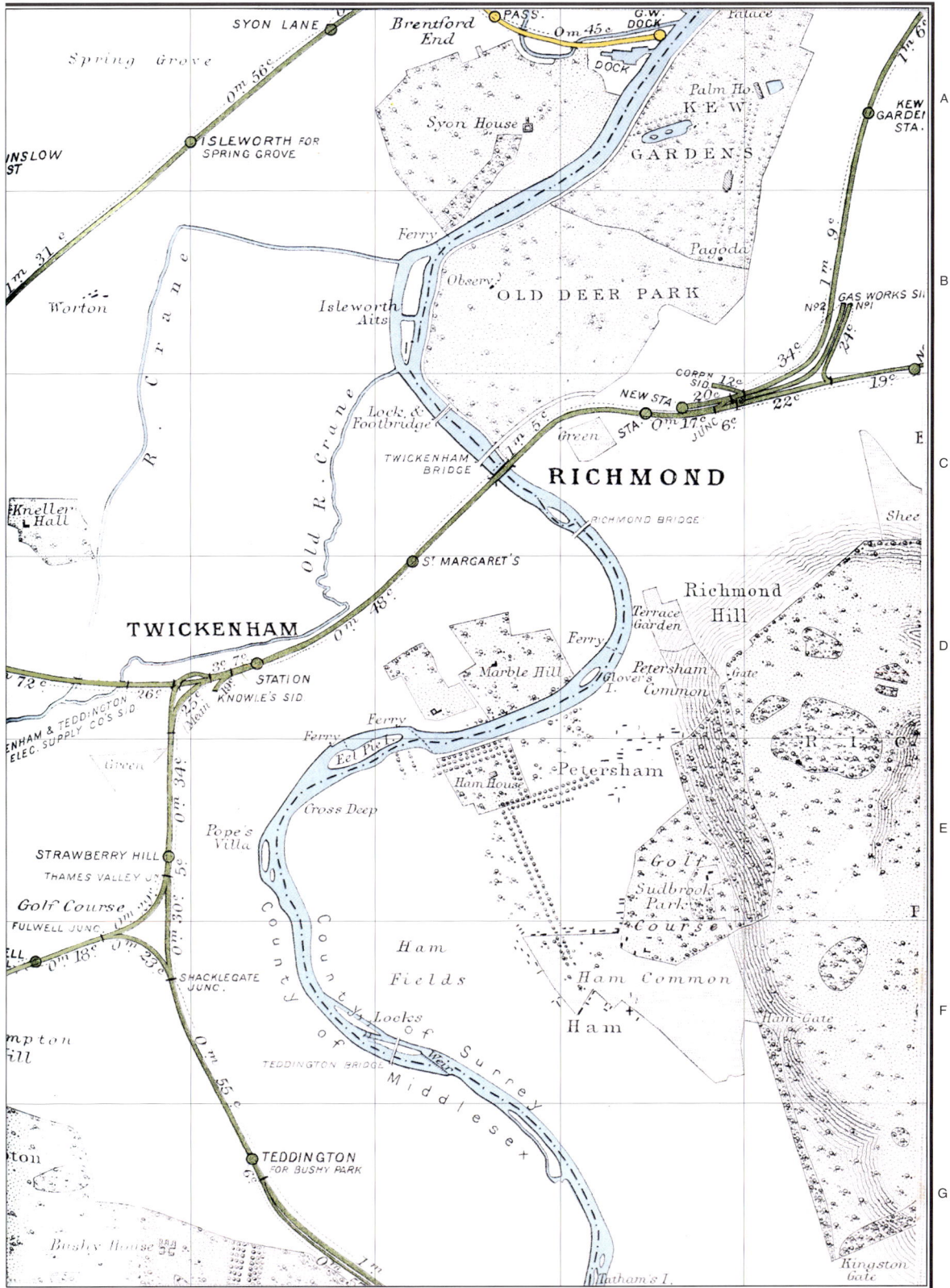

5   4   3   2   1

SYON LANE
Brentford End
PASS.
G.W. DOCK
Palace
0m 45c
DOCK

Spring Grove
Palm Ho
KEW
GARDENS STA.

A

ISLEWORTH FOR SPRING GROVE
Syon House
GARDENS
KEW

INSLOW EST
Worton
Ferry
Observy
OLD DEER PARK
Pagoda

B

Isleworth Aits
GAS WORKS SID
N92 N°1
34c 24c
22c
19c

Lock & Footbridge
Green
CORPN SID 12c
NEW STA
STA 0m 17c
20c
JUNC 6c

Kneller Hall
TWICKENHAM BRIDGE
RICHMOND
Shee

C

RICHMOND BRIDGE

St MARGARET'S
Richmond Hill
Terrace Garden

TWICKENHAM
Ferry
Marble Hill
Glover's I.
Petersham Common
Gate

D

STATION
KNOWLE'S SID.
ENHAM & TEDDINGTON ELEC. SUPPLY CO'S SID.
Green
Ham House
Petersham
R I C

Ferry
Eel Pie I.
Cross Deep

STRAWBERRY HILL
Pope's Villa
Ham
Golf
Sudbrook Park

E

THAMES VALLEY
Golf Course
FULWELL JUNC.
Fields
Course

SHACKLEGATE JUNC.
Locks
Ham Common
Ham Gate

F

mpton ill
County of Surrey
Middlesex
TEDDINGTON BRIDGE
Ham

TEDDINGTON FOR BUSHY PARK
Bushy House
Kingston Gate

G

ton
1m
Tatham's I.

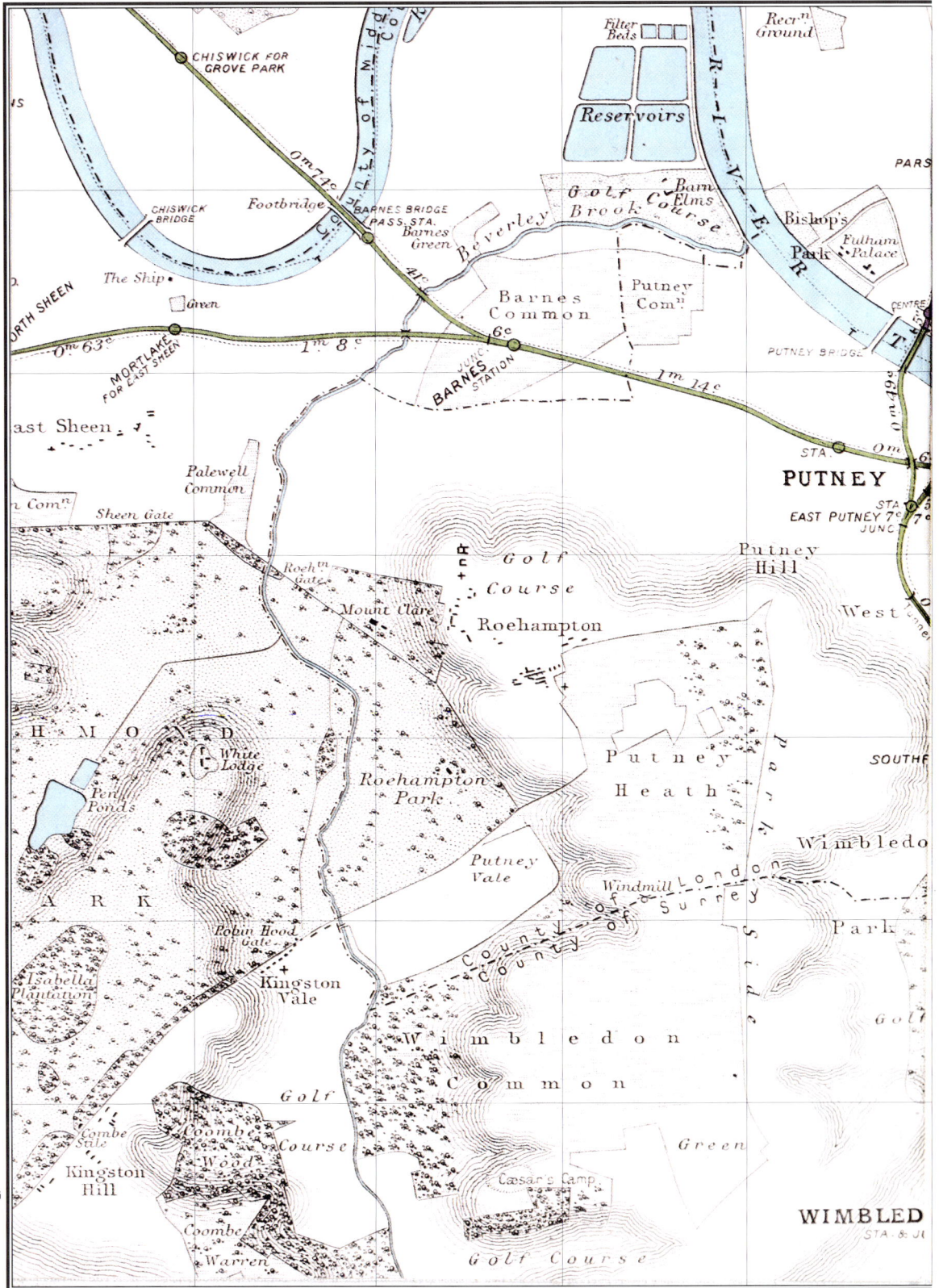

1   2   3   4   5

A

Recr.n Ground

Filter Beds

CHISWICK FOR GROVE PARK

Reservoirs

PARS

CHISWICK BRIDGE

Footbridge

BARNES BRIDGE PASS. STA.

0m 74 c

County of Midd

R - I - V - E -

Golf Course

Barn Elms

Beverley Brook

Bishop's Park

Fulham Palace

B

NORTH SHEEN

The Ship

Green

Barnes Green

41 c

Putney Com.n

Barnes Common

Putney Com.n

CENTRE

MORTLAKE FOR EAST SHEEN

0m 63 c

1m 8 c

6 c

JUNC. BARNES STATION

PUTNEY BRIDGE

T

0m 49 c

East Sheen

1m 14 c

1m 8 c

STA.

0m 6

C

n Com.n

Sheen Gate

Palewell Common

Golf Course

Putney Hill

PUTNEY

STA. EAST PUTNEY 7 c JUNC.

5

7 c

Roeh.tn Gate

Mount Clare

Roehampton

West

D

H M O D

White Lodge

Roehampton Park

Putney Heath

Park

SOUTH

Pen Ponds

E

A R K

Putney Vale

Windmill

Wimbledo

London or Surrey

Wimbledo

Robin Hood Gate

Isabella Plantation

Kingston Vale

County of Surrey

County of London

Park

Golf

F

W i m b l e d o n

C o m m o n

Green

Golf

Combe Stile

Coombe Wood

Golf Course

Caesar's Camp

G

Kingston Hill

Coombe Warren

Golf Course

WIMBLED

STA. & Jt

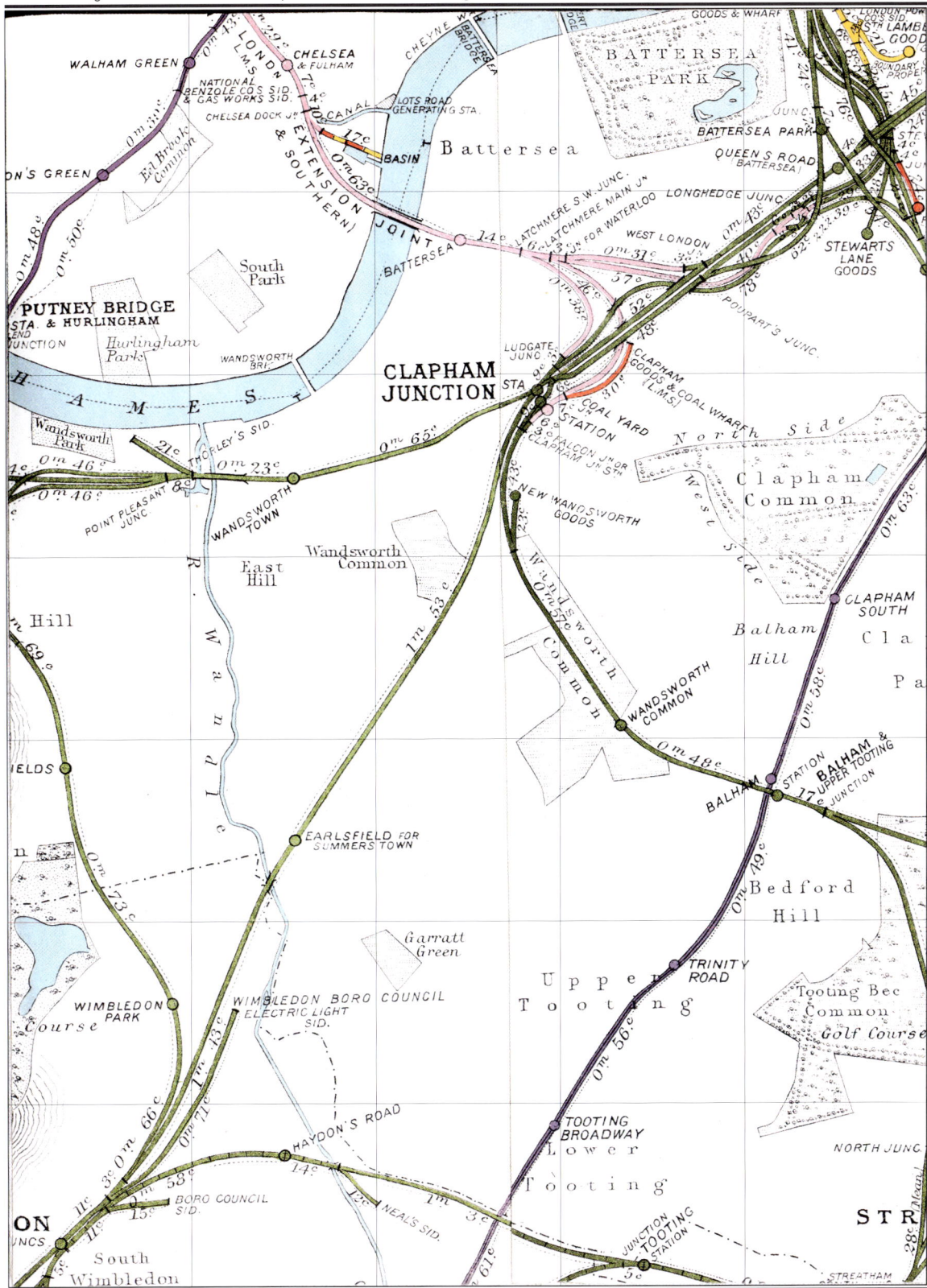

5   4   3   2   1

WALHAM GREEN

CHELSEA & FULHAM

NATIONAL BENZOLE CO'S SID. & GAS WORKS SID.

LOND. (L.M.S.)

CHEESE WRATH BATTERSEA BRIDGE

CHELSEA DOCK JN.

CANAL

17c

BASIN

LOTS ROAD GENERATING STA.

Battersea

GOODS & WHARF

BATTERSEA PARK

BATTERSEA PARK

QUEEN'S ROAD (BATTERSEA)

LONDON POW CO'S SID. 9TH LAMBE GOOD

JUNC.

BOUNDARY PROPER

ON'S GREEN

Ed. Brook Common

0m 30c

0m 48c 0m 50c

PUTNEY BRIDGE STA. & HURLINGHAM END JUNCTION

Hurlingham Park

South Park

WANDSWORTH BRI.

T H A M E S

EXTENSION & SOUTHERN) JOINT

14c

BATTERSEA

LATCHMERE S.W. JUNC.
LATCHMERE MAIN JN.
0m 31c
WEST LONDON

JN. FOR WATERLOO

LONGHEDGE JUNC.

57c

52c
48c

POUPART'S JUNC.

STEWARTS LANE GOODS

CLAPHAM JUNCTION STA.

LUDGATE JUNC.

COAL YARD

CLAPHAM & COAL WHARF GOODS (L.M.S.)

30c

North Side

Clapham Common

West Side

CLAPHAM SOUTH

Cla Pa

Wandsworth Park

THORLEY'S SID.

21c

0m 46c 0m 23c

0m 65c

FALCON JN. OR CLAPHAM JN. STN.

NEW WANDSWORTH GOODS

POINT PLEASANT JUNC.

8c

0m 46c

WANDSWORTH TOWN

R. Wandle

East Hill

Wandsworth Common

Wandsworth Common

1m 53c

WANDSWORTH COMMON

Balham Hill

0m 38c

Hill

0m 69c

0m 48c

BALHAM STATION

BALHAM & UPPER TOOTING JUNCTION

17c

FIELDS

0m 73c

0m 49c

Bedford Hill

EARLSFIELD FOR SUMMERS TOWN

Garratt Green

WIMBLEDON BORO COUNCIL ELECTRIC LIGHT SID.

Upper Tooting

0m 56c

TRINITY ROAD

Tooting Bec Common

Golf Course

Course

WIMBLEDON PARK

HAYDON'S ROAD

TOOTING BROADWAY

Lower Tooting

NORTH JUNC.

ON UNCS.

1m 53c 0m 71c

15c

BORO COUNCIL SID.

1m 73c

14c

12c

NEAL'S SID.

1m 3c

JUNCTION TOOTING STATION

STR

South Wimbledon

5c

0m 61c

5c

STREATHAM

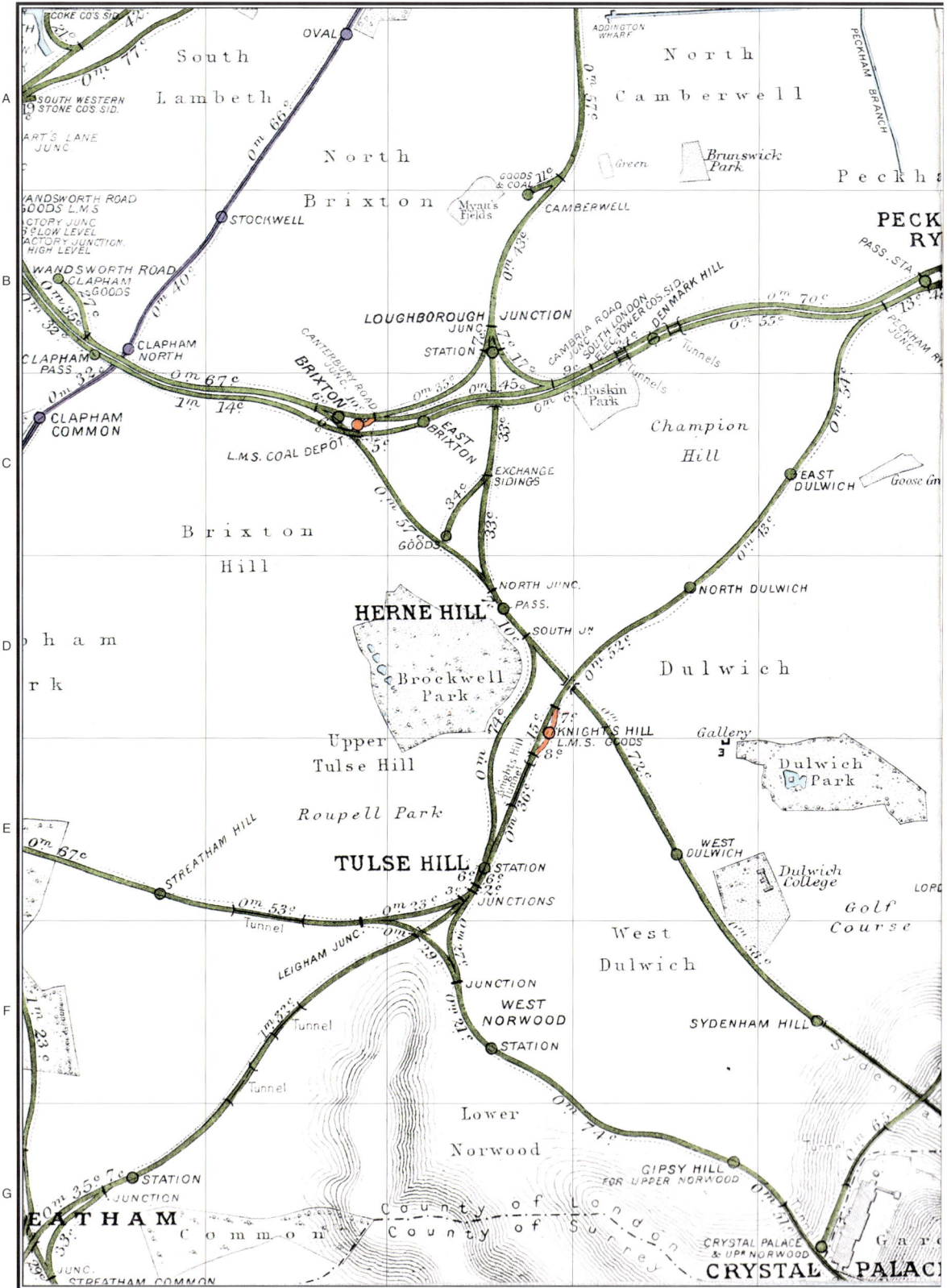

1   2   3   4   5

A

COKE CO'S SID.

SOUTH WESTERN
STONE CO'S SID.

ART'S LANE
JUNC.

South
Lambeth

OVAL

North
Camberwell

ADDINGTON
WHARF

North

Brunswick
Park

PECKHAM
BRANCH

Peckh

B

WANDSWORTH ROAD
GOODS L.M.S
FACTORY JUNC
LOW LEVEL
FACTORY JUNCTION
HIGH LEVEL

North

Brixton

GOODS
& COAL

Green

Myatt's
Fields

CAMBERWELL

PECK
RY

STOCKWELL

LOUGHBOROUGH JUNCTION

JUNC.

STATION

CAMBRIA ROAD
JUNC
SOUTH LONDON
ELEC. POWER CO'S SID.

DENMARK HILL

Tunnels

Tunnels

PASS. STA

PECKHAM RYE
JUNC.

WANDSWORTH ROAD
CLAPHAM
GOODS

CLAPHAM NORTH

CLAPHAM
PASS.

CLAPHAM
COMMON

BRIXTON

CANTERBURY ROAD
JUNC

L.M.S. COAL DEPOT

EAST
BRIXTON

Ruskin
Park

Champion
Hill

EAST
DULWICH

Goose Gn

C

EXCHANGE
SIDINGS

GOODS

Brixton

Hill

NORTH JUN.
PASS.

NORTH DULWICH

HERNE HILL

SOUTH JN.

Dulwich

D

Brockwell
Park

Upper
Tulse Hill

KNIGHT'S HILL
L.M.S. GOODS

Knight's Hill
Tunnel

Gallery

Dulwich
Park

Roupell Park

WEST
DULWICH

Dulwich
College

Golf
Course

LORD

E

STREATHAM HILL

TULSE HILL

STATION

JUNCTIONS

West

Dulwich

F

LEIGHAM JUNC.

Tunnel

Tunnel

JUNCTION

WEST
NORWOOD

STATION

SYDENHAM HILL

Syden

G

EATHAM

STATION

JUNCTION

JUNC.
STREATHAM COMMON

Common

County of London
County of Surrey

Lower

Norwood

GIPSY HILL
FOR UPPER NORWOOD

CRYSTAL PALACE
& UP. NORWOOD

CRYSTAL PALACE

Garde

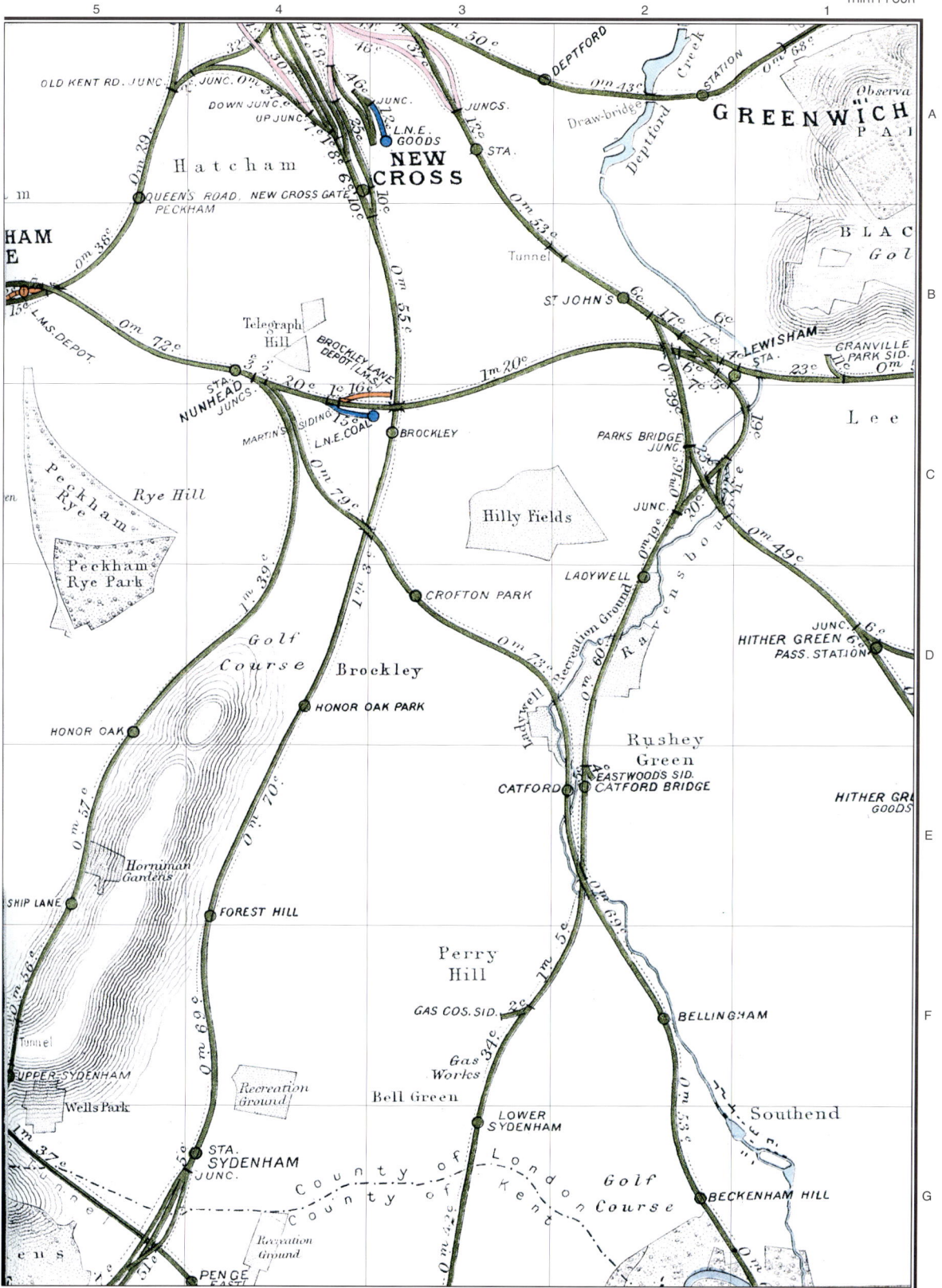

5   4   3   2   1

OLD KENT RD. JUNC.   JUNC. 0m 3c

DOWN JUNC.

UP JUNC.

DEPTFORD

0m 43c

STATION

0m 68c

GREENWICH

Observa

PARK

Draw-bridge

Deptford Creek

A

Hatcham

L.N.E. GOODS

NEW CROSS

JUNC.

JUNGS.

STA.

0m 53c

Tunnel

BLAC

Golf

QUEEN'S ROAD, NEW CROSS GATE

PECKHAM

0m 36c

0m 55c

St. JOHN'S

6c

17c

6c

6c

7c LEWISHAM

STA.

GRANVILLE PARK SID.

0m

B

HAM E

L.M.S. DEPOT

0m 72c

Telegraph Hill

BROCKLEY LANE

DEPOT L.M.S.

1m 20c

23c

Lee

STA.

NUNHEAD

JUNCS.

Peckham Rye

Rye Hill

MARTIN'S SIDING

L.N.E. COAL

BROCKLEY

Hilly Fields

PARKS BRIDGE JUNC.

0m 39c

16c

C

Peckham Rye Park

JUNC.

LADYWELL

Ravensbourne

0m 49c

1m 3c

1m

CROFTON PARK

Recreation Ground

JUNC. 16c

HITHER GREEN

PASS. STATION

D

Golf Course

Brockley

HONOR OAK PARK

0m 73c

0m 60c

Ladywell

HONOR OAK

0m 57c

0m 70c

Rushey Green

EASTWOODS SID.

CATFORD

CATFORD BRIDGE

HITHER GRE

GOODS

E

Horniman Gardens

SHIP LANE

FOREST HILL

Perry Hill

0m 69c

1m 5c

BELLINGHAM

F

Tunnel

UPPER SYDENHAM

0m 50c

0m 69c

Recreation Ground

Wells Park

Bell Green

GAS COS. SID.

2c

Gas Works

39c

LOWER SYDENHAM

0m 53c

Southend

1m 37c

STA. SYDENHAM

JUNC.

County of London

County of Kent

Golf Course

BECKENHAM HILL

G

Recreation Ground

PENGE EAST

0m 42c

0m

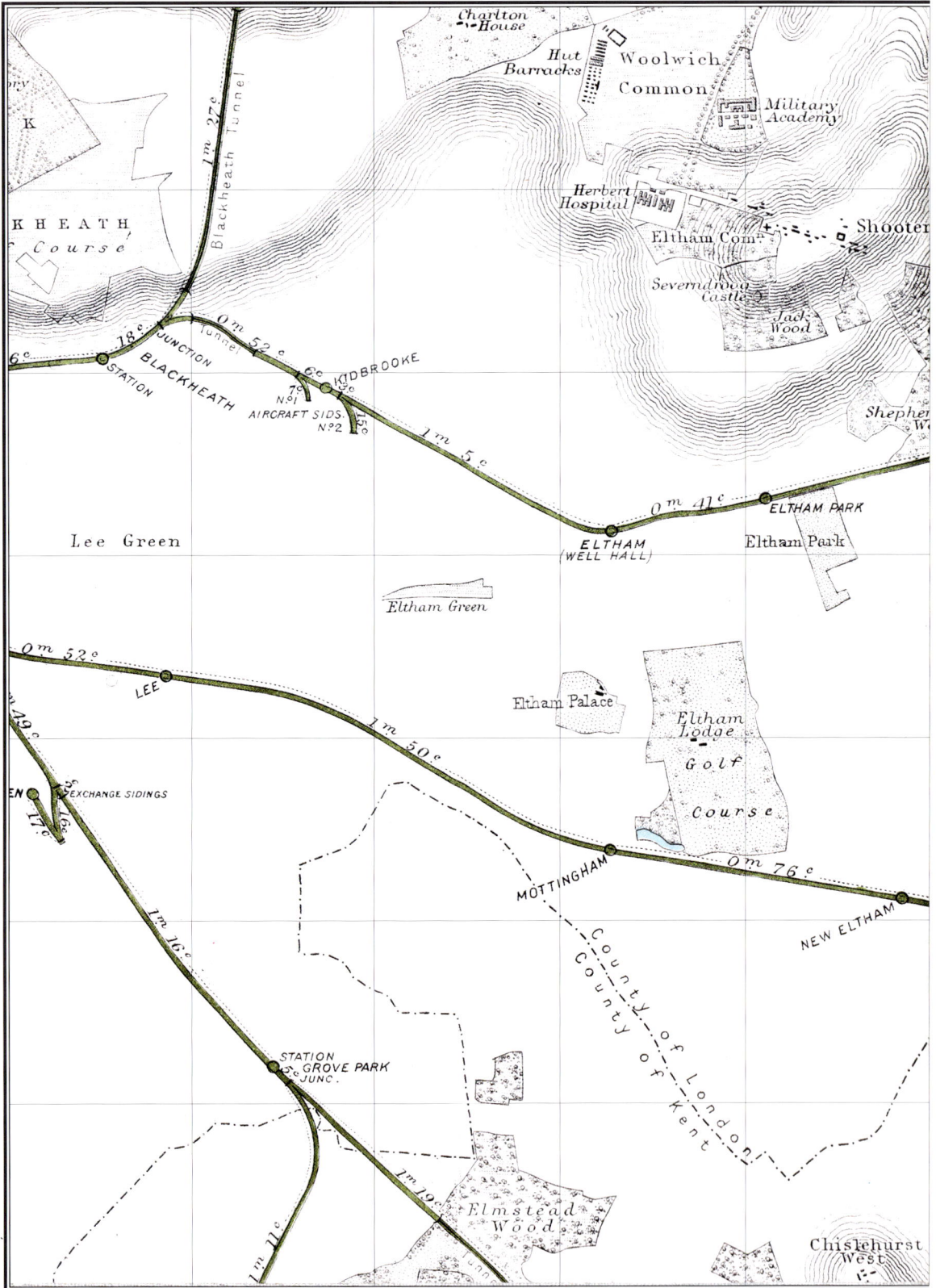

1   2   3   4   5

Charlton House

Hut Barracks

Woolwich Common

Military Academy

Herbert Hospital

Eltham Com

Shooter

Blackheath Tunnel

1 m 27 c

K

KHEATH
Course

Severndroog Castle

Jack Wood

6 c

18 c
JUNCTION
STATION

BLACKHEATH

0 m 52 c
Tunnel

6 c

KIDBROOKE

7 c
N.º1
AIRCRAFT SIDS
N.º2

5 c

1 m 5 c

Shepher W

0 m 41 c

ELTHAM PARK

Eltham Park

ELTHAM
(WELL HALL)

Lee Green

Eltham Green

0 m 52 c

LEE

Eltham Palace

Eltham Lodge

Golf

Course

1 m 50 c

0 m 49 c

EN
EXCHANGE SIDINGS

17 c

MOTTINGHAM

0 m 76 c

NEW ELTHAM

1 m 16 c

County of London
County of Kent

STATION
GROVE PARK
5 c JUNC.

1 m 11 c

Elmstead Wood

1 m 19 c

Chislehurst West

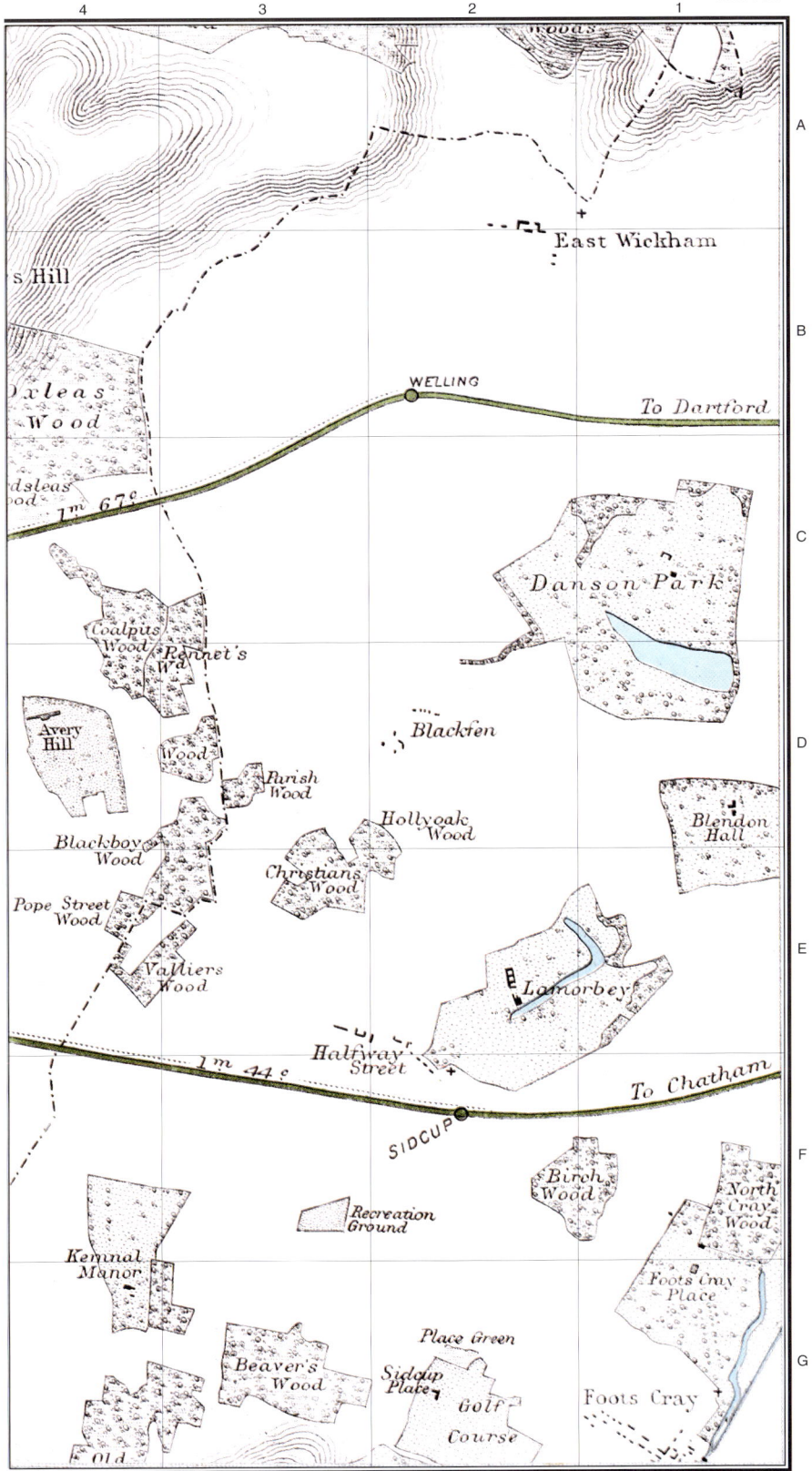

4   3   2   1

A

East Wickham

B

s Hill

Oxleas
Wood

WELLING

To Dartford

dsleas
ood   1ᵐ 67ᶜ

C

Danson Park

Coalpits
Wood   Pennet's
Wᵈ

Avery
Hill

Wood

Blackfen

D

Blendon
Hall

Parish
Wood

Hollyoak
Wood

Blackboy
Wood

Christians
Wood

Pope Street
Wood

Lamorbey

E

Valliers
Wood

1ᵐ 44ᶜ

Halfway
Street

To Chatham

SIDCUP

F

Birch
Wood

North
Cray
Wood

Recreation
Ground

Kemnal
Manor

Foots Cray
Place

Place Green

G

Beaver's
Wood

Sidcup
Place

Foots Cray

Golf
Course

Old

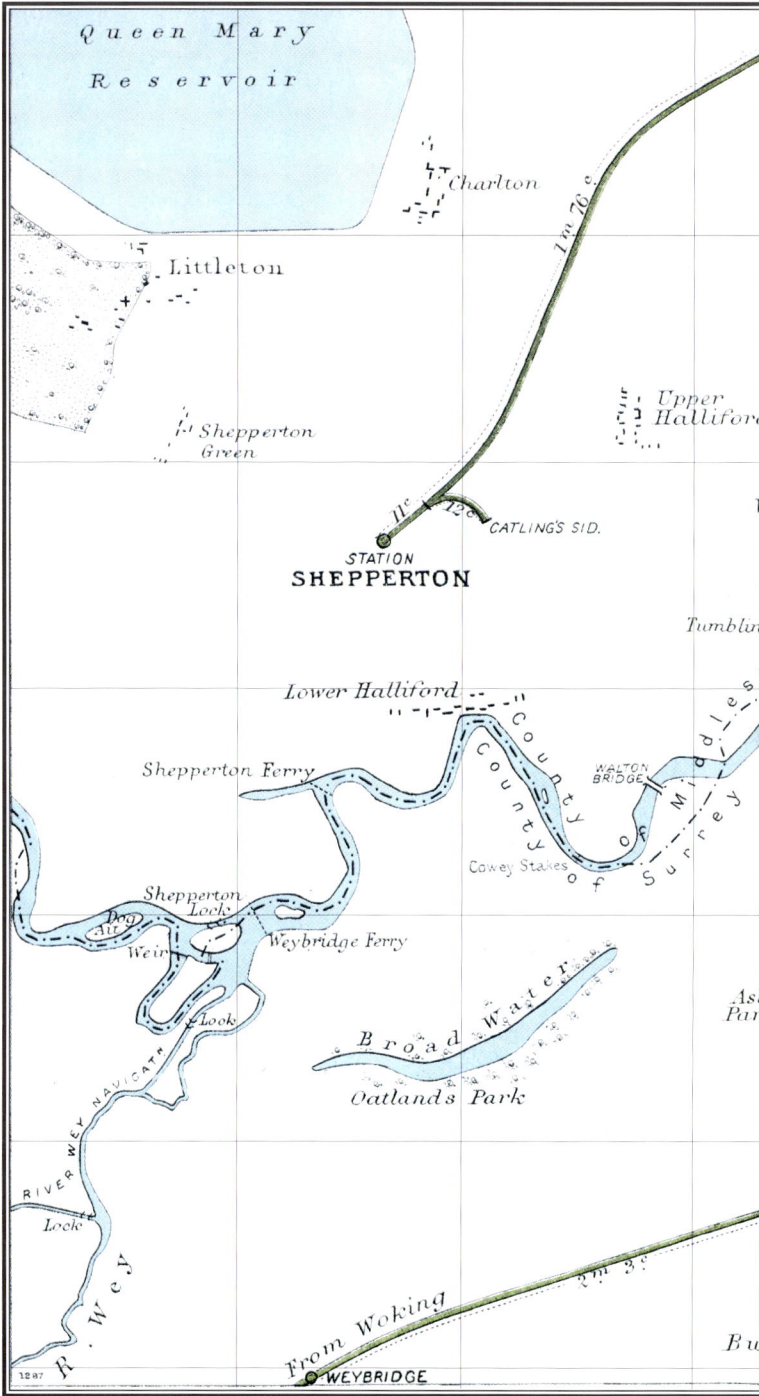

1 2 3 4

A

Queen Mary

Reservoir

Charlton

1 m 76 c

Littleton

B

Upper
Halliford

Shepperton
Green

11 c 12 c CATLING'S SID.

C

STATION
SHEPPERTON

Tumblin

Lower Halliford

County

Shepperton Ferry

of

WALTON
BRIDGE

of Middles

County

D

Cowey Stakes

of Surrey

Shepperton
Lock

Dog
Ait

Weybridge Ferry

Weir

Broad *Water*

As
Par

E

Look

Broad

Oatlands Park

RIVER WEY NAVIGATN

Lock

R. WEY

F

2 m 3 c

From Woking

Bu

G

12 97 ○ **WEYBRIDGE**

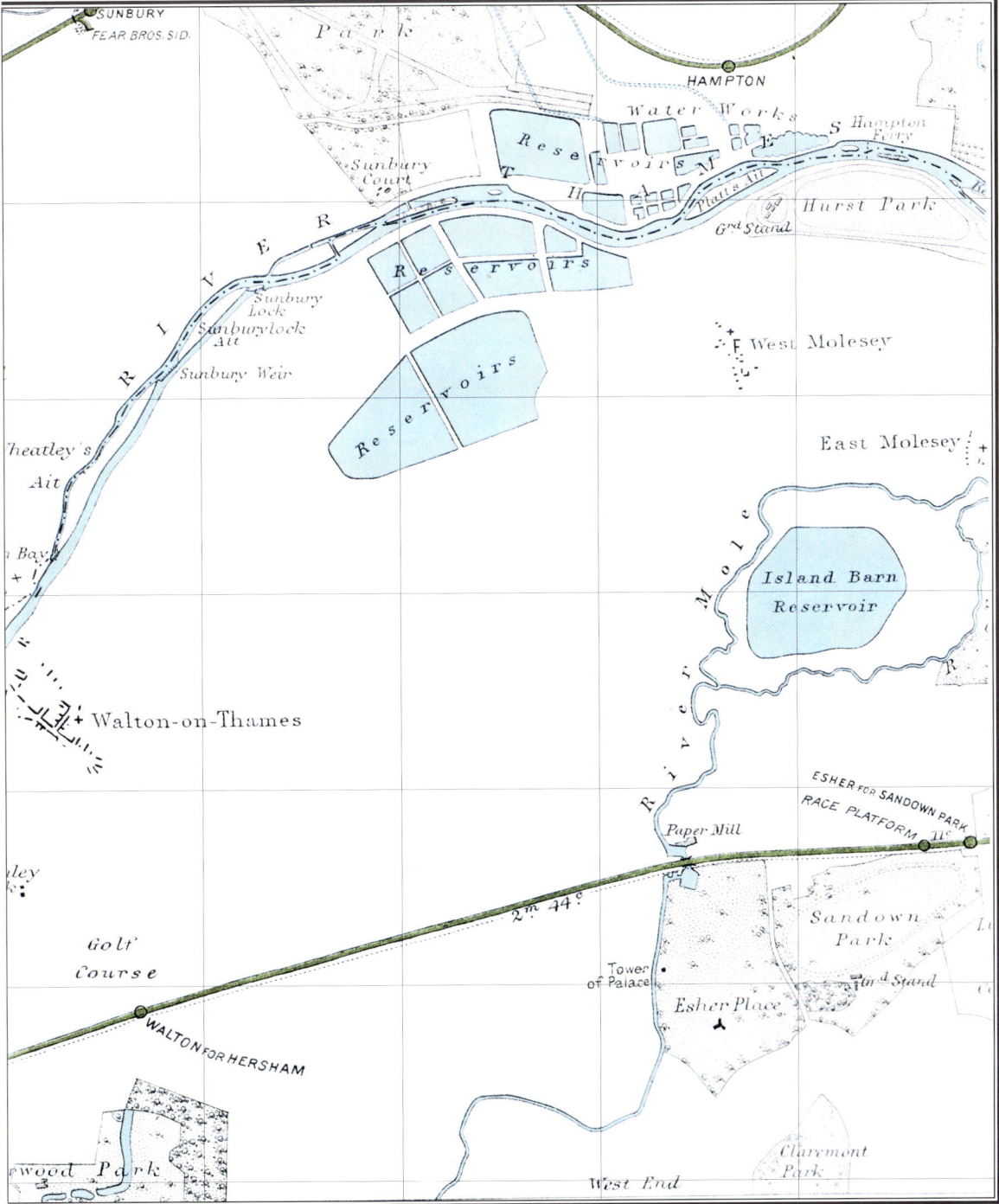

5   4   3   2   1

SUNBURY
FEAR BROS. SID.

P a r k

HAMPTON

A

W a t e r   W o r k s

S Hampton
Ferry

R e s e *r v o i r s*

Sunbury
Court

Platts Ait

Hurst Park

Gr'd Stand

R e s e *r v o i r s*

B

Sunbury
Lock

Sunburylock
Ait

West Molesey

R I V E R

Sunbury Weir

R e s *e r v o i r s*

Wheatley's
Ait

East Molesey

C

Bay.

R i v e r M o l e

Island Barn
Reservoir

D

Walton-on-Thames

ESHER FOR SANDOWN PARK
RACE PLATFORM 11c

Paper Mill

ley
k.

2ᵐ 44c

E

Golf
Course

Sandown
Park

Tower
of Palace

2nd Stand

Esher Place

WALTON FOR HERSHAM

F

rwood   P a r k

Claremont
Park

West End

G

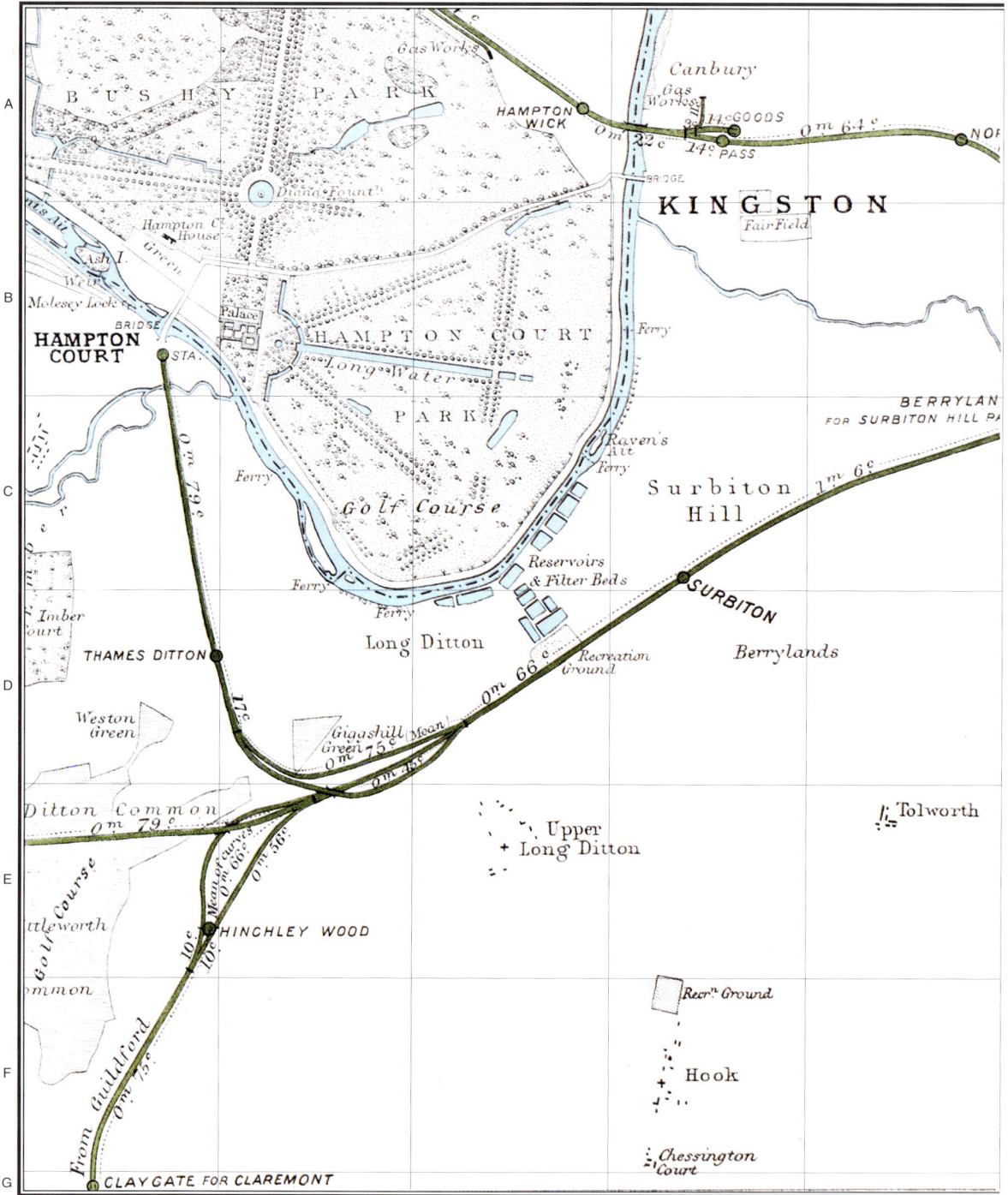

1   2   3   4   5

Gas Works

Canbury
Gas Works

BUSHY PARK

HAMPTON
WICK

14 c GOODS

0 m 22 c

0 m 6·4 c

NOR

14 c PASS.

BRIDGE

Diana Fount.

KINGSTON

Fair Field

Hampton C.
House

Green

Ash I.

Weir

Molesey Lock

Palace

HAMPTON
COURT

BRIDGE

STA.

HAMPTON COURT

Ferry

Long Water

BERRYLAN

FOR SURBITON HILL PA

PARK

Raven's
Ait
Ferry

Ferry

Surbiton
Hill

1 m 6 c

Golf Course

0 m 79 c

Ferry

Ferry

Reservoirs
& Filter Beds

SURBITON

Imber
Court

THAMES DITTON

Long Ditton

Recreation
Ground

Berrylands

17 c

0 m 66 c

Weston
Green

Giggshill
Green

0 m 75 c

0 m 45 c

Tolworth

Ditton Common

0 m 79 c

0 m 56 c

Upper
Long Ditton

Course

Man. or curve
0 m 66 c

ttleworth

10 c

HINCHLEY WOOD

10 c

10 c

Recn. Ground

ommon

From Guildford

0 m 75 c

Hook

Chessington
Court

CLAYGATE FOR CLAREMONT

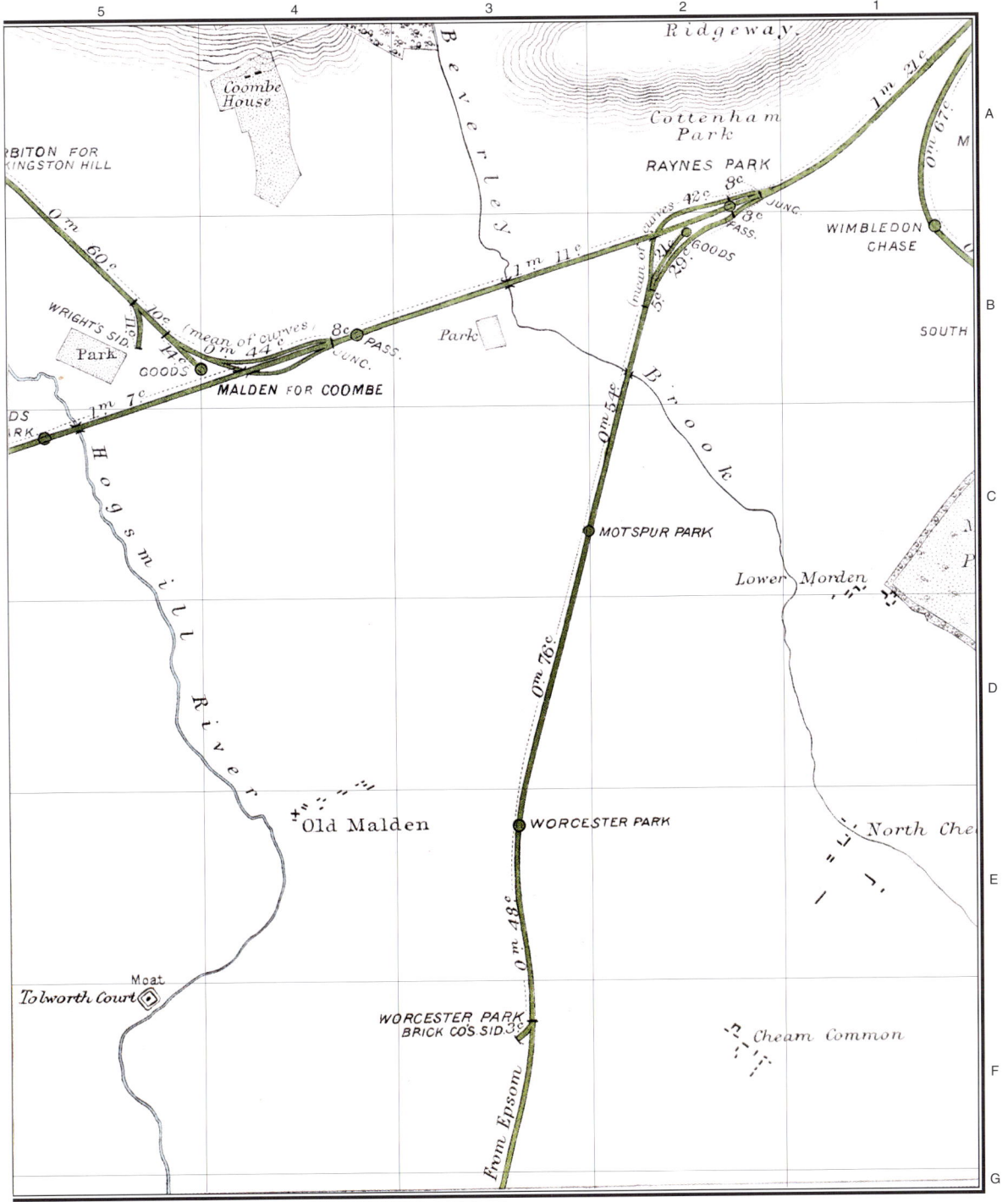

5   4   3   2   1

Ridgeway

Coombe
House

*Cottenham
Park*

A

RBITON FOR
KINGSTON HILL

RAYNES PARK

8c

0ᵐ 60ᶜ

42ᶜ

JUNC.

13ᶜ

WIMBLEDON
CHASE

1ᵐ 21ᶜ

0ᵐ 67ᶜ

M

PASS.

1ᵐ 11ᶜ

Beverley

29ᶜ

GOODS

5ᶜ

SOUTH

B

WRIGHT'S SID.

10ᶜ

11ᶜ

(mean of curves)

8ᶜ

PASS.

Park

(mean of curves)

Park

Park

Brook

Park

0ᵐ 44ᶜ

JUNC.

0ᵐ 53ᶜ

GOODS

MALDEN FOR COOMBE

1ᵐ 7ᶜ

ODS
RK

Hogsmill River

C

MOTSPUR PARK

Lower Morden

P

0ᵐ 76ᶜ

D

Old Malden

WORCESTER PARK

North Che

E

0ᵐ 48ᶜ

Moat

Tolworth Court

WORCESTER PARK
BRICK CO'S SID.

3ᶜ

Cheam Common

F

From Epsom

G

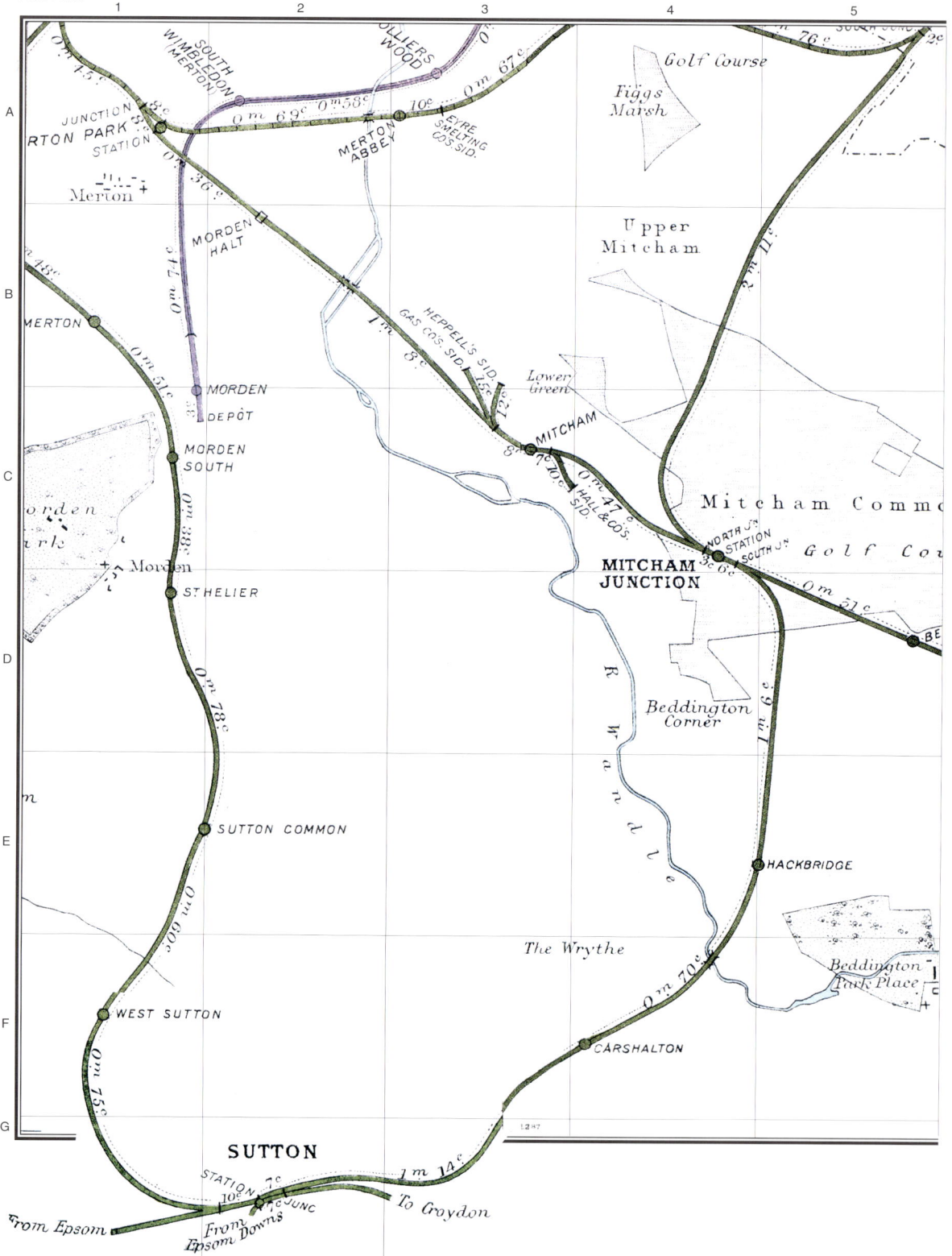

1   2   3   4   5

A

B

C

D

E

F

G

COLLIERS WOOD

SOUTH WIMBLEDON MERTON

Golf Course

Figgs Marsh

JUNCTION STATION

RTON PARK STATION

0 m 73 c.

0 m 36 c.

0 m 69 c.

0 m 58 c.

10 c.

0 m 67 c.

0 m 76 c.

2 c.

SOUTH 2 c.

MERTON ABBEY

EYRE SMELTING CO'S SID.

Merton

Upper Mitcham

0 m 36 c.

MORDEN HALT

0 m 71 c.

2 m 11 c.

MERTON

0 m 48 c.

0 m 51 c.

1 m 8 c.

HEPPELL'S SID.

GAS CO'S SID.

Lower Green

MORDEN DEPÔT

MITCHAM

Mitcham Common

Morden Park

MORDEN SOUTH

0 m 33 c.

8 c.

7 c.

0 m 70 c.

0 m 47 c.

HALL & CO'S. SID.

NORTH Jn STATION SOUTH Jn.

3 c. 6 c.

Golf Cou

0 m 51 c.

Morden

ST HELIER

MITCHAM JUNCTION

0 m 78 c.

Beddington Corner

1 m 6 c.

BE

R
a
n
d
l
e

SUTTON COMMON

0 m 60 c.

HACKBRIDGE

The Wrythe

Beddington Park Place

WEST SUTTON

0 m 75 c.

0 m 70 c.

CARSHALTON

SUTTON

STATION

10 c.

0 m 7 c.

JUNC

1 m 14 c.

To Croydon

From Epsom

From Epsom Downs

5　　　　　4　　　　　3　　　　　2　　　　　1

PASS.

GOODS

0m 33c

27c

0m 36c　NORBURY

Golf Course

Norwood

A

JUNC
LOW LEV.

1m 16c

0m 73c

B

*Recreation
Ground*

1m 0c

21c

18c

GOODS

THORNTON HEATH
PASS.

0m 56c

JUNCTION

0m 23c

0m 50c

0m 26c

0m

C

NORWOOD JUNC
STA. & JUNC & SOUTH N
FOR WOO

Sout

SMITH & SONS
Nor'wo
CROYDON CORP

*Recreation
Ground*

0m 19c

3c

30c

STA.
SELHURST

JUNC.

20c

5c

FORK JNS.

*Woodsi
Green*

D

INGTON
LANE

rse

n

0m 30c

BRITISH P.C. MAN⁵ⁿˢ SID.

0m 42c

2c
2c

4c

STANDARD STEEL
CO'S SID.

METAL PROPELLERS
LTD. SID.

Broad Green

GLOUCESTER R⁴ J⁰
ST. JAMES R⁴ J⁰

23c

0m 6c

17c

33c

22c

0m 53c

0m 40c

0m 57c

WINDMILL
BRIDGE JUNS.

E

PAN BRITANNICA
INDUSTRIES LTD. SID.

*Gas
Works*

7c

22c

GAS CO'S SID.

WEST
CROYDON

STA.
JUNC.

0m 76c

7c

18c

26c

16c

ADDISCOMBE

HALL & CO'S SID.

Beddington

*Recn
Ground*

1m 0c

GOODS

N°1

6c

N°2

EAST
CROYDON
PASS.

F

Mill

*Waddon
Court*

CROYDON

*Park
Hill*

From Sutton

WADDON FOR
BEDDINGTON & BANDON HILL

*Duppas
Hill*　*Halina Park*

0m 73c

From Redhill

From Natal

Tunnels

G

SOUTH
CROYDON

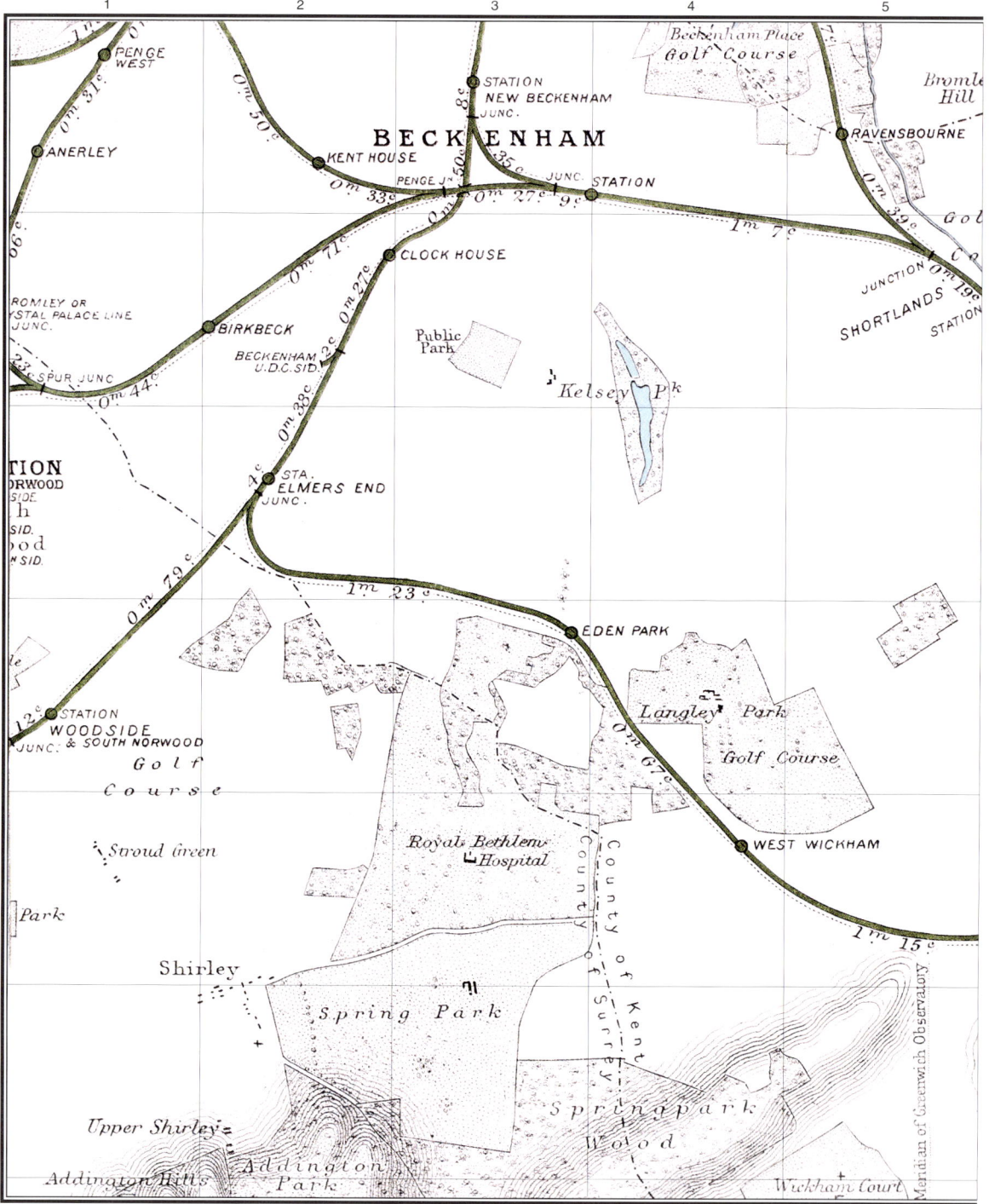

1   2   3   4   5

PENGE
WEST

ANERLEY

Om 81c

1m

Om 50c

0m 90c

STATION
NEW BECKENHAM
JUNC.

0m 8c

BECKENHAM

Beckenham Place
Golf Course

Bromley
Hill

RAVENSBOURNE

A

KENT HOUSE

Om 50c

Om 35c

0m 33c

PENGE J:

JUNC. STATION

Om 27c   9c

0m 39c

1m 7c

Gol
C

CLOCK HOUSE

Om 71c

BROMLEY OR
CRYSTAL PALACE LINE
JUNC.

Om 27c

BIRKBECK

BECKENHAM
U.D.C. SID.

2c

Public
Park

Kelsey P k

JUNCTION   Om 19c

SHORTLANDS
STATION

B

SPUR JUNC

23c

Om 44c

Om 33c

TION
RWOOD
SIDE.

h
SID.
od
N SID.

4c   STA.
ELMERS END
JUNC.

Om 79c

1m 23c

Om 67c

EDEN PARK

Langley   Park

Golf Course

WOODSIDE
STATION
12c

C

JUNC: & SOUTH NORWOOD

Golf

Course

D

Stroud Green

Park

Royal Bethlem
Hospital

County

of Kent

WEST WICKHAM

1m 15c

E

Shirley

Spring Park

County of Surrey

Meridian of Greenwich Observatory

F

Upper Shirley

Addington Hills

Addington
Park

Springpark
Wood

Wickham Court

G

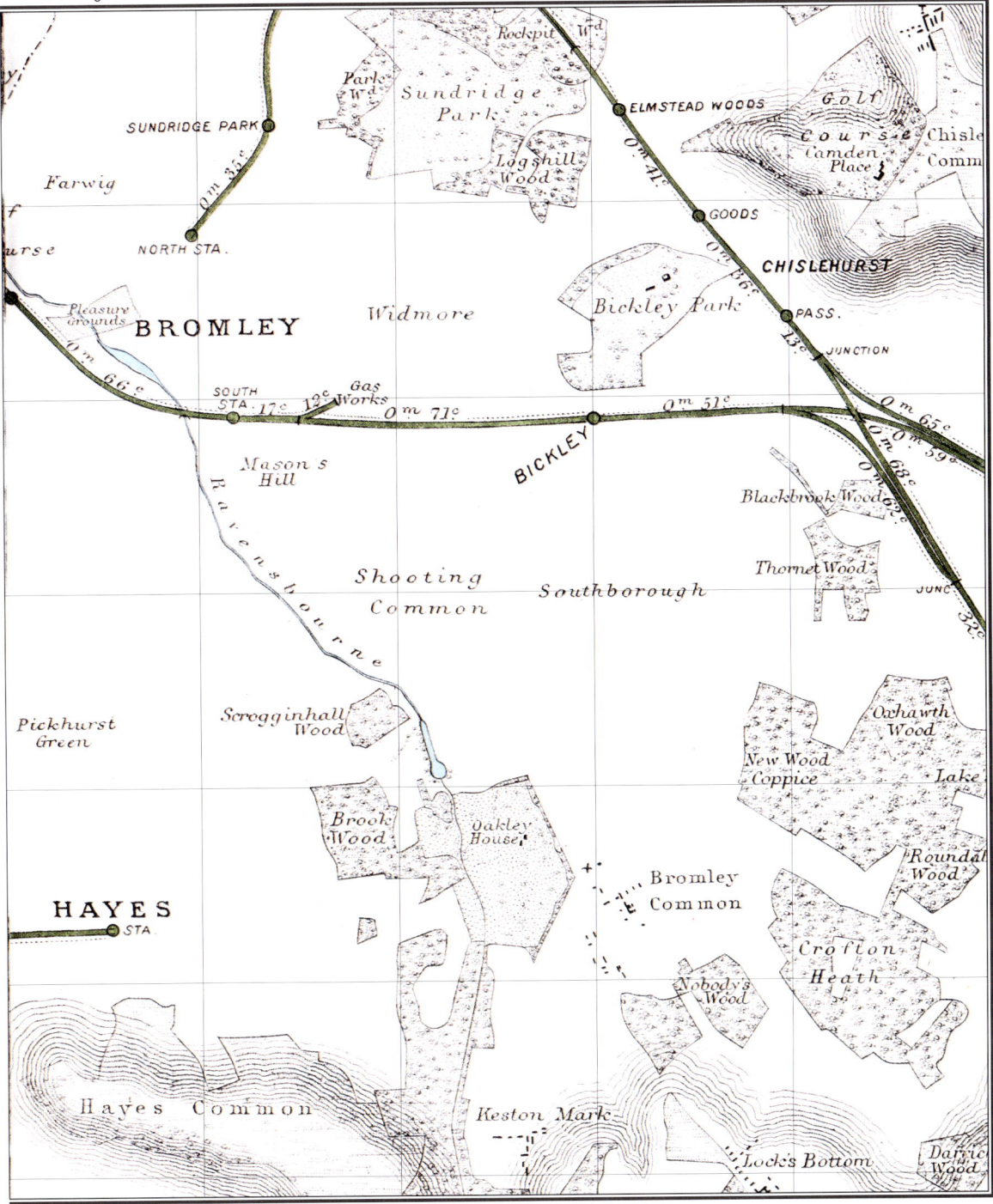

5   4   3   2   1

Rockpit Wd

Park Wd

Sundridge Park

ELMSTEAD WOODS

Golf Course

Chisle

SUNDRIDGE PARK

Logshill Wood

Camden Place

Comm

A

Farwig

GOODS

CHISLEHURST

NORTH STA.

0ᵐ 35ᶜ

0ᵐ 41ᶜ

0ᵐ 46ᶜ

13ᶜ

Pleasure grounds

BROMLEY

Widmore

Bickley Park

PASS.

B

JUNCTION

0ᵐ 66ᶜ

SOUTH STA. 17ᶜ 12ᶜ

Gas Works

0ᵐ 71ᶜ

0ᵐ 51ᶜ

0ᵐ 65ᶜ

0ᵐ 59ᶜ

0ᵐ 68ᶜ

Mason's Hill

BICKLEY

Blackbrook Wood

C

Ravensbourne

Shooting Common

Southborough

Thornet Wood

JUNC.

32ᶜ

Pickhurst Green

Scrogginhall Wood

Oxhawth Wood

D

New Wood Coppice

Lake

Brook Wood

Oakley House

Roundal Wood

E

HAYES

STA.

+

Bromley Common

Crofton Heath

Nobody's Wood

F

Hayes Common

Keston Mark

Lock's Bottom

Darric Wood

G

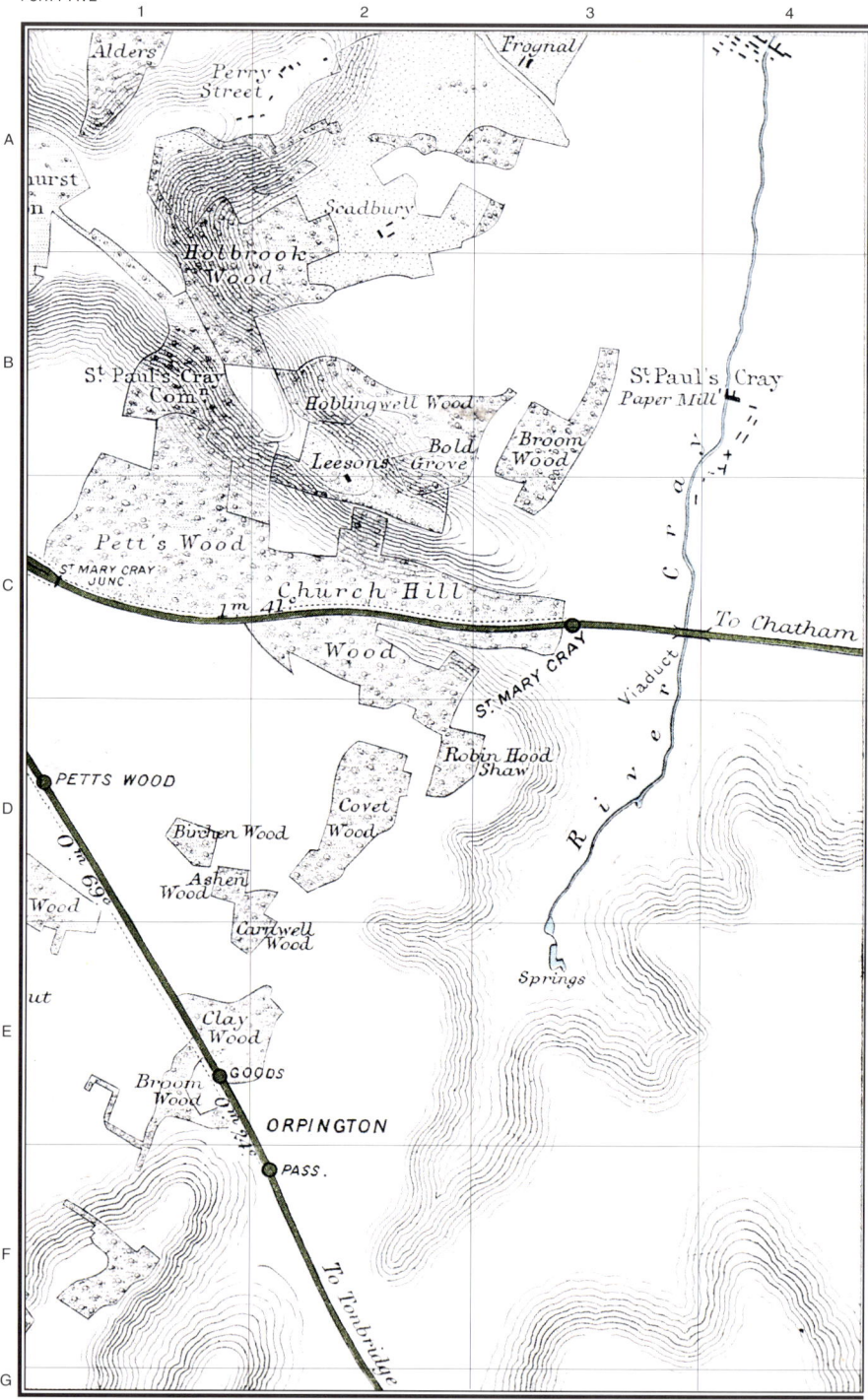

1   2   3   4

A

Alders

Perry Street

Frognal

Scadbury

hurst n

Holbrook Wood

B

St Paul's Cray Com

Hoblingwell Wood

St Paul's Cray
Paper Mill

Bold Grove

Broom Wood

Leesons

Pett's Wood

C

St MARY CRAY JUNC.

Church Hill

1m 41

Wood

St MARY CRAY

To Chatham

R i v e r   C r a y

Viaduct

Robin Hood Shaw

D

PETTS WOOD

Covet Wood

Birchen Wood

0m 69

Ashen Wood

Wood

Cartwell Wood

Springs

E

Clay Wood

Broom Wood

GOODS

ORPINGTON

PASS.

F

To Tonbridge

G

INDEX